GROUPS

UNDERSTANDING PEOPLE
GATHERED TOGETHER

TOM DOUGLAS

TAVISTOCK PUBLICATIONS
LONDON AND NEW YORK

*To Shirley with love and grateful thanks
for all her help and encouragement.*

*First published in 1983 by
Tavistock Publications Ltd
11 New Fetter Lane, London EC4P 4EE
Published in the USA by
Tavistock Publications
in association with Methuen, Inc.
29 West 35th Street, New York, NY 10001
Reprinted 1985*

© 1983 Tom Douglas

*Photoset by Rowland Phototypesetting Ltd
Bury St Edmunds, Suffolk
Printed in Great Britain by
Richard Clay (The Chaucer Press) Ltd
Bungay, Suffolk*

British Library Cataloguing in Publication Data

*Douglas, Tom
Groups.
1. Social group work
I. Title
361.4   HV45
ISBN 0-422-77660-2
ISBN 0-422-77670-X*

Library of Congress Cataloging in Publication Data

*Douglas, Tom.
Groups: understanding people gathered together.*

*Bibliography: p.
Includes index.
1. Social groups   I. Title.
HM131.D655 1983   302.3   83–406
ISBN 0-422-77660-2
ISBN 0-422-77670-X (pbk.)*

CONTENTS

Introduction   1

PART ONE   GROUP PROCESSES

Introduction   15
1   The Attempt to Make Sense of Existence   18
2   The Description and Nature of Groups   29
3   Group Processes   56

PART TWO   THE PROBABLE EFFECTS OF GROUP PROCESSES
IN 'NATURAL' GROUPS

Introduction   77
4   The Family   83
5   Friendship Groups   100
6   Work Organizations   111
7   Teams   123
8   Committees   138

PART THREE   THE PROBABLE EFFECTS OF GROUP
PROCESSES IN THE DESIGN AND FUNCTION OF
SPECIAL ENVIRONMENTS

Introduction   155
9   Residential Institutions   158
10   Therapeutic Environments and Communities   176
11   Specific Types of 'Created' Groups   189

PART FOUR   IMPLICATIONS

Introduction   209
12 A Consideration of Some of the Major Implications   212

References   239
Index   248

INTRODUCTION

In previous books I have attempted to synthesize the known data about social groupwork groups. While doing this it became increasingly clear to me that in reality these groups are only a special case of a larger whole; they are a member of the family of groups. This means that what all groups have in common is probably much more fundamental to the understanding of group behaviour than the differences to which so much attention is given.

As the evidence of similarities piled up, I eventually realized that there are no absolute differences between apparently widely disparate groups. The differences that exist, and there are many, are essentially a matter of degree, even in groups as transient as a chance meeting of people and as permanent as a family. For instance, some of the factors that are ominously present in an angry mob are also present, but in infinitely reduced intensity, in a group of friends, and the power relationships that may be clearly visible and culturally supported in a family group are also in action in a group of children playing in the street.

Where the degree of difference is great there can obviously be a tendency to see the issues involved not as existing on a continuum of intensity or quantity but as separate and distinct entities in their own right. Two such factors that will serve to illustrate this point are time and leadership behaviour.

Time, in relation to the understanding of group behaviour, is a complex factor. In the very simplest sense it is an absolute necessity. If a number of individuals do not spend a certain amount of time in each other's presence then nothing that can be called a group actually exists. While this is essentially true of the initial stages of group formation it is not so true of later stages. Once a group has formed, that is, when its members have spent some time together, then something that did not previously exist has been created and memories associated with it have been generated. It then becomes possible to continue to feel to be a member of the group although not continuously in the physical presence of other members. Being a member of a family, and appreciating the strength of the bonds that such a group can exert even in the long absence of contact, is a common enough experience.

Time is, therefore, an element common to all groups. However, it is also an infinitely variable factor, and the amount of time that is used by different kinds of groups creates enormous apparent differences in the nature of such groups. Some people would maintain that a given period of time in contact is necessary before the people involved become a 'group'. Up to that time the collective nature of their association is given names such as 'grouping', 'amalgamation', or 'transient group', which stress the individual and separate nature of the members' contribution and the lack of a sense of unity or belonging. I would maintain that this apparently huge difference to a 'formed' group, aware of its unity probably more than of its members' individuality, is a matter of degree and that the major factor involved is time. Given more time in association, the difference between the formed and unformed group will be lessened.

Other factors are crucial and time is not always the most essential. But certainly without sufficient time these other factors are not able to bring about change. In essence that change is a diminution, or enhancement, a redirection of factors that already exist as part of basic human interaction patterns. Time is not an absolute factor in the differences between groups but a constant with consequences dependent upon the degree of its availability and use.

Leadership activities are frequently advanced as a major, if not the most important, factor in defining the nature of a given group. Thus, the choices that the leader makes about what will take place are seen as determining what kind of group will emerge. A very obvious example of this lies in the apparent dichotomy of leadership that is usually expressed as directive/non-directive, or as leader centred/group centred. It is assumed that groups on one side of the dividing line are different from those on the other. There are differences, but the choices available to either kind of leader are not infinite and, moreover, are the same for any group. What a leader chooses to emphasize and use does not eliminate the effect of the factors not selected, though it may alter the power of their influence. If a leader chooses to work with individuals in the context of a group, it will certainly produce a group very different in appearance and possible achievement from a group operated by a leader who chooses to use his or her skill to create an awareness on the part of the members of their own power, responsibility, and resources. In either case, the factors not chosen for emphasis are still there and are creating effects, however diminished.

In essence, therefore, leadership acts, whether performed by selected individuals or by all the members of a group, do not create absolute differences, only a difference in the degree to which some of the available factors in group behaviour are given precedence over others. This leads to the realization that there is no such thing as a leaderless group; there are only groups with different degrees of leadership residing in the actions of one person or several.

If all groups have a limited number of factors that can be influenced and that have influence, then the stage can be set for the development of a wider understanding of group behaviour that is not dependent upon starting from approaches or viewpoints outside the idea of the 'group' as an entity in its own right. The similarities of all human groupings can be shown to reside in an identifiable number of variables that are ubiquitously present, but in differing intensity and importance, wherever human beings are gathered together.

The main reasons for writing this book, then, are to identify more clearly than before the ubiquitous factors that have been called group processes, and to give examples of their presence in several different forms of human associations in order to generate an awareness of the influences that tend to determine human social behaviour and its outcomes, and also to increase the probability of controlling these by the exercise of conscious choice over known elements, a choice that did not exist when these elements were operating covertly.

A second reason for writing is that for a long time people have sought to create groups for beneficial purposes and their energies and understanding of group behaviour have been directed to this form of group. In a very real sense this has directed attention from the groups that already exist and are hugely instrumental in shaping and controlling our lives. I want to try to divert some of this attention to a recognition of existing group situations where the same skills that are essential to the 'created' group can be used for less obvious but equally useful and productive groupwork.

The family is an exception. Its essentially grouplike nature has long been recognized and to some extent this is also true about work groups, although the idea that work organizations are group structures and subject to group dynamics is of relatively recent recognition. This leads us to a consideration of the context within which this book is set.

THE CONTEXT IN WHICH THIS BOOK IS SET

'In my opinion, scientific psychology is potentially one of the most revolutionary intellectual enterprises ever conceived by the mind of man. If we were ever to achieve substantial progress toward our stated aim – toward the understanding, prediction, and control of mental and behavioural phenomena – the implications for every aspect of society would make brave men tremble.'   (Miller 1969b : 1065)

Miller's presidential address to the American Psychological Association in Washington in 1969 was devoted to 'psychology as a means of promoting human welfare'. Miller constantly emphasized the underuse of data concerned with human behaviour and the continued acceptance of techniques, ideas, and understanding that had been shown at best to be often inaccurate and, at worst, to be wrong to the point of being counterproductive. One of his main concerns was to discover who was responsible for attempting to bridge the gap between the discovered and discoverable data and the techniques of human interaction.

Research data in the physical sciences seep across into everyday life through industrial techniques probably because there is a fairly obvious connection between the data and the prospect of making money. Apart from being of an essentially different nature to that available in the physical sciences, data about human behaviour do not seep across in anything like the same way. There are two particular reasons for this: first, there is no immediately obvious profit motive. The second reason relates to the attitude that people in general have to discovered information (that is, available data, e.g. research or other forms of systematic collection of information) about human behaviour. This sort of information appears infinitely more disputable, and, if believed, more threatening, and yet most people who would admit to being ignorant about chemistry have few qualms about claiming a fair knowledge and understanding of human beings.

The disputable nature of research data about human behaviour

If an astronomer says there are probably a million other planets in the universe that are identical to earth, then while the average person may not wholeheartedly believe such a statement, they are not likely to dispute it. There are many reasons for this. There is no direct or abiding effect set up by this piece of knowledge on the everyday life of the average person. While the information may be interesting, its impact is minimal except for those who already have an interest in the subject for one reason or another. Now, if a scientist says that he or she has measured the standard mile and found it to be six inches too long, then the dispute that may arise has a very practical bias because measuring is something that most people feel they know something about and they can actually test such claims for themselves.

If a behavioural scientist makes any comment about human behaviour the data can be challenged both on the basis of involvement (the challenger is human and to that extent involved), and on the basis that his or her estimate of the situation will very often be very different from that of others. Also, most people have a strong belief that human beings are unpredictable and almost certainly not reasonable in the behavioural sense except in terms of crude statistics.

The threat involved

If human behaviour can be measured, or worse still if it can be predicted, then each of us becomes that much more knowable. In our society there is a great suspicion of those professionals, for example psychiatrists and psychologists, who are apparently endowed with the ability to see and understand more than others. We can protect our secret selves, our hidden thoughts, and our generally unknown behaviours only by maintaining that claims 'to know' are largely spurious and to be discounted.

This kind of refusal is often buttressed by the nature of the information that behavioural scientists have at their disposal. This tends to be either so general that it appears irrelevant to the layperson, or, if precise, is concerned with such a minute area of behaviour as to appear irrelevant in wider context. The very nature of research into human behaviour is significantly different to that conducted in the physical sciences. For example, no behavioural scientist can experiment with material to anything like the same extent, and, moreover, on the few occasions when subjects are submitted to controlled experiments, this raises outcries about ethical behaviour and the results are likely to be dismissed because the circumstances were 'artificial' and not 'natural'.

Most people have learned to equate scientific method with the method of the physical sciences and to apply that kind of standard to the behavioural studies with eminently dismissive consequences. Andreski, for example, suggests that:

'More than that of his colleagues in the natural sciences, the position of an "expert" in the study of human behaviour resembles that of a sorcerer who can make the crops come up or the rain fall by uttering an incantation.'

(Andreski 1974 : 24)

Admittedly many behavioural scientists also fall into this trap and attempt to increase the scientific validity of their work by quantifying their results. Often such data are meaningless, but a scientific gloss has been achieved and challenges can be met by data that borrow the certainty of a physical science, i.e. mathematics.

The knowledge of being human

Essentially this factor relates to an extremely potent bias. Most of the phenomena that physical scientists discuss lie outside the human being. The individual is aware that these phenomena are neither other human beings nor part of his or her own being, and aware that it would be difficult to claim either knowledge of or familiarity with most of these factors – unless, of course, the individual has special knowledge and experience, in which case he or she will clearly recognize this.

But behavioural scientists are talking about a subject they know very well. They are talking about human beings and so about *themselves*! The basic 'facts' upon which scientific theory is promulgated are as well known to the behavioural scientist as to the researcher. Now a strange double-think becomes apparent. Statement one: 'Because all human beings are so individualistic, their behaviour cannot be quantified'. Statement two: 'BUT because I am a human being I know a great deal about all other human beings because of our common humanness'.

These statements are not as exclusive as they appear at first sight and even if they were, for the purposes of this argument it would be irrelevant. What is relevant is that both are the sources of resistance to data about human behaviour that goes far beyond the bounds of rational caution.

Obviously, without abandoning necessary caution, a way has to be found of reducing resistance to the use of data in this sphere. In essence, this probably means a kind of translation process based on familiarity with both sides of the fence and that is really where this book lies. It attempts to provide the necessary translation for one particular area of behavioural science, namely group dynamics. In a sense this task is easier than the endeavour to translate some other behavioural studies because there is a great interest in group behaviour and equally a great appetite for information that can underpin either understanding or techniques of intervention.

One of the major tasks of this kind of 'translation' process is the need to use different kinds of language to express the different nature of the concepts. This will be dealt with later. It is sufficient to say here that the essence of effective translation is to put into an understandable language the very nature of what was originally couched in terms devoid of meaning for the average person. While the symbols have been changed, the essential meaning stays the same.

One further point needs to be made. Those who struggle to understand human behaviour, for whatever reason, need information that can be used and adapted to techniques of practice and not those used only in an experimental situation where factors are controlled to enable the result to be deemed valid. The kind of data required must illuminate actual situations, offer the possibility of clearer understanding, and, finally, not only suggest what actions are appropriate but also provide a range of methods and techniques for pursuing them.

Most of what has been said so far has presented only part of the case. For instance, in many situations total lack of understanding of the language used is infinitely preferable to a state in which understanding is felt to exist and yet does not. Total lack is both a real and easily recognizable state. It can be dealt with as a practical issue, i.e. steps can be taken to improve understanding or the project can be abandoned as useless. Both are essentially real responses to a real situation. Where understanding is deemed to exist and yet does not, any action based on it is based on false assumptions and in that sense cannot be founded in reality.

The problem of understanding will be dealt with later. But it is likely that readers of a book such as this are already partially committed to some of the ideas it contains. Those who will not read it if asked would probably comment on its irrelevance or, worse still, describe it as 'common sense'. Both comments are clear enough indications of the sort of knowledge barrier that exists in the field of human behaviour and the limited possibility of reaching the uncommitted.

THE WAY THE BOOK IS SET OUT

Part One starts very simply by adducing reasons why anyone should be concerned with the ways in which people behave in group situations and is designed to look at the problem of what constitutes understanding and acceptable explanation. Having looked in general terms at these factors (which are very important because if two people who wish to communicate with one another start from different concepts of understanding and explanation, their attempts to understand each other are doomed for apparently inexplicable reasons), I then describe in some detail the actual factors that are the main concerns of this book, that is, groups and group processes. In particular, group processes, which are readily recognizable in action but not as readily or as easily translated into instruments of analysis, are looked at from three major standpoints: as a function of interaction, of group influence, or of communication. What tends to emerge is their ubiquitous nature and thus their value as indicators of what is actually happening. Having presented the idea of group processes it is then necessary to show that they exist in groups that in the scientific sense very often are not usually seen as 'groups' but merely as spontaneous collections of people gathered together over longer or shorter periods of time for more or less specific purposes.

Part Two looks at families, friendship groups, work organizations, teams, and committees, with the express purpose of analysing whether the form of each group designed to accomplish such different aims and purposes is brought into being because different group processes are emphasized in each structure.

If this is true then the design of the so-called 'natural' groups should offer a range of possible design factors that can be adopted in 'created' groups with maximum efficiency in generating the kind of outcomes for which such groups were brought into existence. This would indicate the existence of a large range of selectable factors that in a very specific sense had either long- or short-term 'known' outcomes. Of course, as many other variables may not be known with equal clarity (e.g. the past experience of group members), the element of the unknown remains high. However, the focus and efficiency of groups designed on these bases need to be considerably improved.

Part Three sets out to provide evidence for this assertion by investigating how group processes, seen as design factors, are used in various 'created' group situations. If the thesis is correct then groups that use specific purpose-achieving processes with conscious direction and attempt to reduce the impact of specific purpose-negating processes should be the most effective in achieving their defined goals.

However, non-achievement may be equally suited to our required proof if it can be shown that some 'created' groups and community organizations fail either because negating factors were ignored or because such factors were too all-pervasive or powerful to be effectively reduced. In either case, we have evidence that 'created' groups can only be as effective as the degree of cognizance taken of the processes and constraints involved.

Part Four moves back to non-'created' groups and attempts to consider the effects of group behaviour in certain areas of social behaviour not usually looked at in this way. All social behaviour – even that which occurs in isolation from other human beings – is basically group oriented. Much of what appears to be as inexplicable in our behaviour to others may well be understandable, or at least more so, if analysed in group–process terms. In this fourth section the possible implications of the operation of group factors are looked at in social behaviours as apparently widely separated as mental illness and learning.

THE AIMS OF THE BOOK

The aims of this book should now be clear. In a word, they are to explore the operation of group processes in human assemblies, and to try to demonstrate their ubiquitous nature.

The aim must therefore be to attempt to increase the possibility of understanding social situations by reducing them to the causes that reside in the operation of group processes. Of equal importance is to try to show that when a group is created for a specific purpose it can be 'designed' in the sense that what is known about the ways in which 'natural' groups function can be used to ensure the most beneficial outcome for the especially 'created' group. Inevitably, it must be among those who have to deal with the problems and casualties of our society that such understanding should develop. However, I would rather see such understanding grow in ordinary people and thereby obviate the growing dependence on the so-called expert who is so characteristic of our time.

A third aim must be to show that even without understanding on the part of those involved, the pressures in any group situation will still operate. The focus, intensity, and selection of those pressures by group members will depend not on any rational choice but upon the lessons directly and indirectly learned from past experience of similar situations of whatever nature. This may well be parochial knowledge at its worst, partial, biased, and founded on limited and possible self-safety seeking behaviour, i.e. behaviour whose purpose is to maintain or increase the sense of personal safety in any social situation. No rational choice about the most efficient method of pursuing outcomes can be decided upon when little of the necessary data to make such a decision is in the hands of those involved.

This kind of situation has often been seen as one of the main factors in the establishment of traditional patterns of response that largely preclude the possibility of either wrong perceptions or changing circumstances being taken into account. The generation of stereotyped responses ensures the partial failure of many group enterprises, characterized by entrenched behaviour, attitudes, and beliefs, and by the bringing into play of routines of interaction that are most clearly categorized by the fact that they have been set in the past and tend to be regarded as sacrosanct. The overall effect of such procedural straitjackets ensures not only that any outcomes are strictly limited and relatively unsatisfying, but also that no one has been taken advantage of.

This leads to the fourth and final point of this introduction. Suspicion, distrust, and the sense that one is about to be taken advantage of, all rest on many possible causes. But ignorance is one of the principal factors involved: ignorance of the ways in which advantage can be taken, and ignorance of the methods by which protection by understanding, rather than by being merely heavily defended and obstructive, may well be its two major forms.

People simply do not see what is happening around them except perhaps when their own safety is threatened, or, most usually, when their own personal interests are at stake. It is not surprising, then, that people whose experience, natural bent, or training have taught them to see what total movements and sub-movements are taking place and what the outcomes are likely to be, tend to be seen as arch-manipulators. The term 'manipulator', with its pejorative connotations, can only be justified if their understanding is deliberately hidden and utilized for their personal gain.

So, the fourth aim is to attempt to sow the seeds of recognition, to see what is going on, because only then can autonomous decisions be made that begin to utilize some of the potential awareness of human beings.

PART ONE

Group Processes

INTRODUCTION

'all men are engaged in trying to make sense out of the
world around them, and trying to check the sense they
have made by noting its predictive capacity.'
(Bannister 1969 : 895)

It seems to be a characteristic of human beings that some
perceptible order is necessary both to our understanding and our
sense of security. What is predictable in the sense of being
knowable, however terrible, is much more acceptable than what
is unknown, which seems to provide the basis for much human
fear. Using this as a starting point, not only is it possible to see all
human exploration as an attempt to know about ourselves and
our environment in a way that categorizes, lists, formulates, and
demonstrates connections between things, but our more immediate daily functioning also does much the same.

Comfort and security reside in the ability to predict, or more
accurately, in the belief that prediction is possible. When the
unexpected occurs we are not happy until we have offered and
accepted some form of explanation for its occurrence. If the
necessary data are either inadequate or non-existent then data
from similar occurrences are used in an attempt to explain or
understand the occurrence and to reduce the fear induced by an
unexplained happening.

One of the very basic explanations offered about human
behaviour is founded on common humanity. If A does this to B
then C explains A's behaviour to his or her own satisfaction
by saying that A being human, like C, behaves in much the
same way C would behave in like circumstances. Sometimes this

assumption about the causes of A's behaviour is modified by the fact that C has an extensive knowledge of A, and probably of B, and of the circumstances in which they interact. The degree to which such modification is possible varies enormously from person to person and situation to situation. No one has the time, or indeed the inclination, to acquire the knowledge required about even a small number of the people with whom we have daily dealings.

Although most of this is commonplace and reasonably well accepted, strangely enough this acceptance does not serve to modify our behaviour very much, and neither does it lead to a ready acceptance of such statements. Each human being inhabits a separate and unique world that overlaps those of others to only a variable degree but which is seldom total except under unique circumstances, and even then usually only for very short periods of time.

Thus, a frustrating dichotomy emerges. We need to perceive order in everything around us and within us but our ability to perceive, especially where other human beings are concerned, is, or tends to be, distorted by the way our perceptual mechanisms function. In order to eliminate personal bias we experiment, holding some variables constant and gauging change in others; we count occurrences and try to eliminate bias by using vast numbers, statistical analyses, and other gambits that reduce the probability that individual predilection has skewed the result. The results, as far as human behaviour is concerned, are either so general or so minute as to be useless in practice, or else there is a reversion to speculation and imaginative proposition that then lacks quantifiable justification.

The group processes, constraints, and other factors outlined here are based on the assumption that if a sufficient number of people describing events produce what appear to be identical concepts, then there is likely to be some foundation for making sense of what they are describing. In order to eliminate the possibility that their descriptions emanate from an area of common overlap in their otherwise unique worlds, it is obviously better if the descriptions are separated by time and place and are given by describers who do not all come from exactly the same background. Most of the work of analysing these descriptions has been done in a previous work, which is used as the basis for the present analysis (Douglas 1979).

1

THE ATTEMPT TO MAKE SENSE
OF EXISTENCE

INTRODUCTION

'At all levels of thought we, and probably all other species that
possess any awareness, operate by setting up and testing
hypotheses, by solving problems and selecting strategies. And
this applies to attention, perception, imagery and memory, as
well as to the non-conscious weighing of evidence that we
exercise in matters of judgement and belief. This means that
there can be no such thing as objectively right or identical
answers. Even the laws of nature are subject to conscious
interference, and no two individuals can ever experience anything in the same way.'   (Watson 1979 : 252)

We live in individually unique worlds, a fact that tends to be
obscured by our insistence on similarities. However, if the
common nature of all human beings is taken to be all-
encompassing then many irreconcilable differences of perception
and understanding have to be categorized as conscious acts of
will, which is obvious nonsense. Even such simple acts as
describing a colour are subject to individual interpretation. Each
individual receives the same stimulus but the way in which what
is seen is communicated to others depends on the individual
collection of data and the uses to which it is put. For instance,
when we want to match colours we place them side by side in the
same light if possible, especially if other people are involved in
the process of selection. We know that description under these

conditions is subject to wide variation of interpretation and therefore is not reliable.

If this applies to one visual stimulus, i.e. wavelengths of light, then how much more difficult an achievement is the common interpretation of complex pieces of human behaviour, especially when the observer is directly and actively involved. However, so effective is the accommodation that we have learned to make, that in general we are irritated, enraged, or pitying about the lack of agreement of perception in others. It is as if identical perception is an absolute, while difference is some form of failing.

There are some fairly powerful influences at work here. The essential fear of isolation of all human beings is mitigated by being accepted by others; similar beliefs and ideas draw people together and reduce the isolating sense of difference. Accepting particular perceptual interpretations also brings the comfort of one's perceptions being confirmed by others.

The adaptation we make must be one of acceptance, the *as if* adaptation. We take a given datum *as if* it were absolutely true and base our procedures upon this. A different accepted base line strikes us as wrong. If it is powerfully supported it threatens our position, while if it is weakly supported we can resist it, scorn it, and try to put it down. Thus, we live in a world not of certainties, but of points of reference that are not absolute and immovable, but fixed by an agreement to accept that this is what is.

Heisenberg's (1927) principle of uncertainty shows that the more detail we seek the more there is to seek, and seldom do we come to anything that remains steadfast under all forms of scrutiny. We are faced with the prospect, not of knowing, but of accepting a workable sense, a usable order, about human existence. It is the problem of agreeing what kind or degree of sense is acceptable as much as different levels of readiness to accept or different levels of intelligence that confounds understanding.

I am aware that this is an argument for generalities rather than particulars as the basis of agreement and that it is also an argument based on utility. However, if those generalities take the form of recurring patterns and if the expectation of those patterns and recognition of them generates the ability to use them in modifying experience, then I for one am happy to accept that this is a step forward from the generally accepted thesis of the non-predictability of human behaviour. It makes sense of existence in a way that is far from being either theoretically or rigorously refined, but yet allows us to work with human situations with a degree of consistency of outcome and flexibility of approach that cannot be obtained otherwise.

Trying to make sense of existence is a technique of imposing a pattern upon observed data that produces a *modus operandi* that squares with the data appropriately enough to facilitate our performance. As new or changed data become available so the patterns will change. It must also be possible to create different, more particular, or more general patterns for particular needs in the sense that any pattern can be split down further into its component parts to infinity and any pattern can be incorporated in a larger encompassing one, also to infinity.

The purpose of this text is to take a set of patterns that have already been roughly defined and to show that understanding of some social situations can be enhanced by their extension and application to social groupings of varied kinds. In the process the patterns may require some modification. They may, for instance, become more refined without thereby losing practicality, or they may also be seen to form part of larger patterns. But because the claim is that recognition of these patterns can lead to increased understanding of the situations in which they occur and thus to a new possibility of intervention whether it is used or not, it is necessary to look briefly at the thorny problem of what is an acceptable pattern of understanding.

UNDERSTANDING

'We are constantly taking information given in one form and translating it into alternative forms, searching for ways to map a strange new phenomenon into simpler and more familiar ones. The search is something we call "thinking"; if we are successful we call it "understanding".'   (Miller 1969a : 49)

'No psychological process is more important or difficult to

understand than understanding, and nowhere has scientific psychology proved more disappointing to those who have turned to it for help.'   (Miller 1969a : 90)

The Concise Oxford English Dictionary includes the following definitions of 'understanding':

1 Comprehend, perceive the meaning of;
2. grasp mentally, perceive the significance, explanation, cause or value of; know how to deal with;
3 infer, especially from information received, take as implied, take for granted;
4 supply word mentally (for example, expressed or under-stood).

Elsewhere in this book (p. 214) Scheflen (1974) is quoted as saying that actions have no meanings in themselves; any meaning resides in the context in which the action occurs. Miller (above) seems to be saying that understanding resides in an ability to describe a new phenomenon to ourselves in familiar terms. The more complex the new phenomenon happens to be the greater the difficulty we may have in relating it to previously understood concepts that would generate understanding; total lack of comprehension equates with total lack of familiarity.

But another point has to be made here that complicates the picture. It is one that is a constant source of problems in all forms of communication, namely the acceptance of understanding as existing when, in truth, little or no real understanding is there at all. Acceptance of this nature is more problematic than lack of understanding that may be obvious in its absence, first because it may be taken as a true register of the state of knowledge by others, but, more importantly, because the assumption that knowledge exists precludes any need to search for it.

With regard to group behaviour, it is quite clear that most people in their everyday lives have some understanding of some of the dynamics. There are great differences in understanding, and there are some traditional reasons that are accepted that are neither wholly false nor wholly true. But there are large areas of group influence and behaviour patterns that are not only ascribed to wrong causative factors but are not even consciously appreciated at all.

A common enough example of this is the way decisions are made in a group. Although most of the members of the group will have contributed to the decision that is reached, unless the process was remarkably clear and simple (for example, one person dominating the whole discussion and compelling a decision on his or her terms), then few members will be clear about how the final decision was made. Some of this uncertainty must lie in the inability of group members to be actively involved in discussion and yet be aware of what is happening to the group as a whole. Involvement of this nature tends to focus perception almost exclusively on supplying the needs of being so involved. However, it is also true that observers, who are not involved, can only ascertain a little more of the process if they have a frame of reference, an instrument by which they can order and assess the impressions they receive.

This book is directed towards creating such a frame, though in a very real sense such a frame has already been created and it is its use in the generation of understanding that concerns us here. The maze of complex variables that constitute a group interaction has to be referred to some base for understanding. What matters is that this base is consistent and, perhaps more important, logically structured, neither so simple as to be ridiculous nor so complex as to be unusable. In practical terms this means something that falls between the micro processes of the individual behaviours and the macro processes of the intergroup relationships.

Understanding is a prerequisite of efficient use. Without it, any intervention in a group system must at the best be guesswork or the reproduction of previous, learned behaviour stimulated by apparent recognition; at the worst it is sheer blind chance. Whatever schema one uses to understand complex phenomena, there is always the possibility that other, more effective schemata exist, if only one knew about them. But we are in the very early stages of attempting to understand how groups of human beings function and are very far from even being able to contemplate how many factors might be involved, except in very broad terms, in just a simple piece of group behaviour. In this case we are looking for understanding that can underpin practical use and not understanding for its own sake as an intellectual exercise.

THE COLLECTION OF DATA

'psychologists, scientists in other fields, and laymen confront the same problems in their attempts to understand the world. Successful coping behaviour requires appropriate perceptions, the creation of which involves selection of information, organisation and supplementation of existing data with references.'   (Medcof and Roth 1979 : 28)

'Perhaps it is one of the deepest subtleties of consciousness that you are able to see things without getting involved. When you get involved you don't see.'   (Postle 1980 : 31)

The first part of any exercise to increase understanding of group behaviour must be to collect as much information as possible about the ways in which groups have performed and to see what similarities emerge. Here one runs into snags not only in terms of the diversity of information available – unsystematically collected for many different reasons – but also in terms of the methods by which it was collected and the reliability of the collectors. This is not to denigrate such people, but simply to illustrate that the reason they gathered their information may well not have required any truly efficient validation.

So at one extreme there are simple records of 'what happened', made by people who were actually involved in the events described either actively or as observers. At another extreme we have experimental data in which a given variable of group behaviour is isolated and examined in a way derived from scientific method. Small pieces of behaviour have been measured in terms of the frequency of their appearance, the timing, and the effects. So the range of data is vast, extending from minutely recorded particulars to large-scale generalizations. Often enough, stress has been placed upon the irrelevance of the experimental data because of the 'artificiality' not only of the situation being examined but also of the group that is used.

'Irrelevance' is, I submit, the wrong word to use. The data obtained by experiment have validity to a high degree for the group situation in which they were obtained, and the charge of irrelevance is not really directed at this. Rather, it is aimed at the extrapolation of the experimental finding to all groups without qualification. But, as all groups have essentially the same dynamic bases, the irrelevance cannot be total. It is a question of the degree of relevance that any experimental data have for other groups where the factors affecting outcome and behaviour, though identical in nature, are present at probably very different levels of intensity and usage.

The problem, then, with data collected from any point on the possible range is to discover the degrees of relevance generated by the constellation of factors affecting the described group, that is, to decide, in effect, if there is a general principle that can be discussed in what must always be a situation where the element of uniqueness is a very powerful factor. For this reason attempts to quantify are unrewarding and often futile. The fact that an individual in a recorded group behaved in a particular way so many times is just as likely to be because of his or her sense of being recorded as to any other dynamic in the group process. So perhaps the information about such a group should be recorded as the behaviour of people collected together in such a way, believing such to be their objective, and aware of being observed and recorded!

It is safe, therefore, to deal at a given level of generalization, neither so specific that data relating to extremely isolated details of behaviour are held to be common occurrences, nor so wide that no practical value as a guide to the actual reality of group behaviour can be drawn from it. The kind of generality most often used is described as a pattern or constellation of minor events. Two factors are associated here: first, frequency of occurrence, and, second, what might be called 'consequence'.

That a group is a dynamic entity, constantly changing, means that very seldom do any really fixed points of reference occur, but certainly probability would ensure that some factors seem to occur similar enough in form to be recognizable, with a frequency that permits a level of expectation of their occurrence. These recognizably similar occurrences may be seen to have a detectable relationship to subsequent events, which is not to say that they are causative, but only that there appears to be a sequential relationship. These factors are the patterns of group behaviour and they constitute the sufficient level of generalization with which it is possible to deal.

THE CREATION OF LOGICALLY CONSISTENT EXPLANATIONS (LCES)

'The explanation of thinking requires that we pursue three complementary lines of enquiry; we need concepts dealing with physical and neurophysiological processes, abstract models to handle implicational relations, and genetic concepts to explain how such implicational thinking develops.'

(Bolton 1976 : 42)

In a word, 'logically consistent explanations' are patterns that have a good degree of fit with the available data. In the case of this book, the available data consist of investigators' reports of various relevant aspects of group behaviour. It has already been said that most of this kind of material comes from research into groups that have been set up for purely experimental reasons (that is, to test the existence and function of a piece of group behaviour), and that the amount of material available about groups operating in a 'natural' state tends to be scant.

Not only is such information scarce, it also tends to be of a different character to the data available from experimental groups. The main factor of difference is that it is largely descriptive, in a sense, elaborate case studies of individual examples, whether 'individual' here means one person or one institution. Of course, case studies can be compared but they are seldom, if ever, directly comparable and so the validation of the data produced has to remain at the level of possible explanation rather than mathematical significance, that is, generally applicable, explanation.

However, correlations between observations do exist and they are occasionally supported by other methods of collecting data, for example, statistical data and, more infrequently, experimental findings. What I have tried to do here is to create a category of explanation that I have called 'logically consistent'. Basically this implies that when a piece of information about some aspect of group behaviour recurs in the available data with a reasonable degree of frequency, then I make an assumption that either all the informants have copied one from another, which is unlikely, or they are all describing something remarkably similar. If these similar pieces of data, from whatever source, can be squared with an explanation of what they represent without that explanation being either fantastic or illogical, then probably that explanation will form a logical basis first for understanding the data involved and, second, for pursuing further investigation.

Given the difficulty of investigating 'natural' situations from many points of view, such as observer effect and the almost impossible task of trying to measure what is occurring, it is suggested here that data that have the corroboration of their validity in their being placed in the context of similar data have more value for practical use than either no data at all or the empirical assumptions made in individual situations. Guetzekow uses the terms 'social engineer' and 'technician':

> 'The social engineer is the broad-gauged middleman who knows how to transform basic knowledge from the various social science disciplines into usable forms. He differs, too, from the technician (the pollster in business and industry for example) whose competence is restricted and who may be only slightly familiar with the fund of basic knowledge underlying his specialisation.'   (Collins and Guetzekow 1964 : 3)

Of course, an operational definition must be behind the use of this form of explanation and in this case there are two.

First, when not subject to a group-conscious form of control with deliberate and aware intent to manipulate, collections of human beings produce group behaviour patterns that maximize the achievement of group ends. Second, this process of maximization can be understood in terms of the group processes and 'factors-affecting'.

The logic of this is that groups must be effective at least to some degree because human beings continue to form and reform groups for various purposes. Thus, if it is possible to discover what processes and 'factors-affecting' are prevalent in certain 'natural' groups with given ends, then we may have a clear correlation between certain processes and group consequences. Such a correlation should clearly be of use in two ways:

1 To understand how 'natural' groups work.
2 To be able to design 'created' groups efficiently to perform a required function or functions. To create an efficient and successful 'social engineer'.

Problems concerned with the acceptance and use of LCEs

'it is in language that an expectation and its fulfilment make contact.'   (Wittgenstein in Bolton 1976 : 207)

One problem arising from logically consistent explanations concerns language. In a very rough sense this can be summed up by saying that as we try to broaden experience from the individual incident, through the collection of similar incidents to the extraction of a general theory about such incidents, the language that is essential to embrace and define the necessary concepts has to change. If this process of necessary change is not understood, then fundamental misconceptions easily arise and the value of all parts of the process to those involved is diminished by lack of understanding and appreciation of the nature of each contribution.

The language of everyday life is rich in some ways and extremely banal and impoverished in others. Its function is to facilitate social intercourse and to form a medium of communication about things that are essentially common enough experiences to us all. When special needs arise then a language that is more specific and more accurately defining is needed, and the words used have to be harder and more precise. Such a language change has to take place when something relatively unusual has to be talked about. In a society like ours, where feelings are not often clearly 'owned', then strong emotions are often accompanied by a level of frustration caused by the inability to express them. We often have little practice at expressing emotions and consequently have a limited and limiting vocabulary to express strong or unusual emotions. Grief is an excellent example.

In the same way, a special form of language has to be used when events that occur as isolated experiences are collected together and their similarities and differences quantified. One step away from the individual incident, which itself may have been unusual enough to warrant description in a language not totally part of everyday usage, comes the assertion of general principles. The language here is quantitative and no single incident from the collection used to compile the general principles fits the prescription exactly.

When the next stage occurs, which is the formulation of basic theory, the twin processes of language, change and abstraction, have proceeded even further. General theory provides statements that are held to be universally true and thus uses a language that is conceptual and general; its relationship to the actual incidents on which it was originally founded has become quite tenuous. This 'distant' connection forms the basis of much criticism of so-called theory. It is deemed to be useless because it is either too vague or too general. Logically consistent explanations, which are precursors to general theory, are often similarly defined.

The problem lies in the nature of focus. This can be looked at from two points of view. First, where an individual working with people requires information about how to deal with the situations he or she encounters, his or her focus is upon the practicality of his or her needs. The focus is narrowed and defined by the situation. If the information he or she is offered is wide and general, then unless he or she can alter the focus, it is likely to be rejected as useless. Second, the problem can be resolved by a process of translation in which the generalized theory can be turned into action principles applicable to a given situation by someone with a foot in both camps of practice and theory.

2

THE DESCRIPTION AND NATURE OF GROUPS

INTRODUCTION

'a group should be conceived of as a system whose parts interrelate.' (Gahagan 1975 : 98)

Much has been written about groups, especially over the last thirty years when the all-pervading nature of 'group' influence on human behaviour has been increasingly recognized. The number of words in the English language that have arisen to describe forms of collectivity, both in animals and men, is legion. This is a fair indication of the need to distinguish these groupings and is also a clear mark of the acceptance of their universal nature.

The very general nature of human groupings poses a problem for those who wish to examine group phenomena in more detail. Manifestly ubiquitous group pressures producing some form of conformity and therefore acceptable behaviour, are as little thought about as breathing. In turn this tends to relegate such group pressures to a level below conscious awareness unless circumstances change and unfamiliarity breaks the habitual patterns. This process allows individuals to assume that they make decisions about the trivia of everyday life in ways that are both personal to them and not subject to outside influence whereas the opposite is more nearly the reality. Whatever choices the individual makes, these are already circumscribed by group influences; the less awareness there is of these influences, the more circumscribed the choice and the greater the lack of awareness.

In a very real sense, then, attempting to describe what actually happens when people are gathered together is an effort to delineate more aspects of human interaction, because even actions that are essentially private can, with little effort, be shown to be influenced by group behaviour and, in particular, to be the expected responses of others. It is not too difficult to present an argument for the 'learned' nature of most of human behaviour, nor to argue that it was learned because it produced relatively satisfactory results somewhere in our past experience. In other words, it was behaviour that found acceptance by those who were perceived as important, to us in some way and that thereby brought some degree of satisfaction to us as producers of such behaviour.

Nothing seems more important in the understanding of group influence than the enormous effort that all human beings seem to make to offset any perception they may have of their essentially isolated state. However much human beings involve themselves with others, each is still basically a self-contained unit with no direct, unimpeded link with any other human being (unless he or she is one of a set of Siamese twins). An individual cannot communicate thoughts and feelings without translating them into some form of arbitrary and systematic code, nor can the feelings and thoughts of another be appreciated without the same translation process taking place at both transmitting and receiving ends.

Furthermore, it would seem that not only is the human being isolated in this way but in other ways also. For example, there is the problem of identity, and the constant need for stimulation from other similar beings. Both these factors seem essential to the maintenance of a mentally healthy individual. Our perception of the kind of people we are rests largely on our recognizing the responses we evoke in others. We cannot evoke such responses if our behaviour is so unacceptable that we are excluded from the company of others. Similarly, unless we receive sufficient response from others, we cannot be socially competent individuals.

While there are other factors involved, we are concerned here to make explicit only the functions of group influence in everyday life. The reasons for so doing are simple enough and reside in the concept of a human being as a thinking animal. By 'thinking' I mean a process of conscious assessment of the factors involved in any situation and also an assessment of the nature of the equipment we possess for making such assessments. Choices can only be made if an awareness of alternatives and their value exists at the moment of decision making. Some choice almost always exists. But in many circumstances the hidden influences that over- or under-value a choice, or even obscure a possible alternative, limit any selection and thus affect the outcome.

Such hidden influences, which stem mainly from group pressures, can be made more explicit by the expedient of acquiring some understanding of the way in which groups operate. By increasing understanding of the function of group influence, erstwhile hidden influences become manifest and any decision can be more widely and accurately based.

Definitions of dynamic entities such as groups present many difficulties but it is hoped that the description offered here will provide a reasonable basis for the widening of understanding about groups in general.

THE ARBITRARY NATURE OF THE 'GROUP' CONCEPT

'A group is . . . the largest set of two or more individuals who are jointly characterised by a network of *relevant* communications, a shared sense of collective identity and one or more shared goal dispositions with associated normative strengths.'
(Smith 1967)

In one clear sense a group is a purely arbitrary distinction, the nature of which may be very important when certain kinds of groups are studied. All groups are collections of human beings. What determines the degree of 'groupness' must be at a very basic level, for example, the amount of time they spend in each other's company. Thus, if people congregate for noticeable periods of time then they lose some of the fluidity of a haphazard gathering. The observer can say they are an elementary or rudimentary group. Social life is composed of just such groups.

The arbitrary nature of such a definition is marked by the fluctuations of perception of observers. For example, observers may disagree about the sufficient minimum time needed for a rudimentary group to be established. Thus, some researchers set purely arbitrary levels about how much of any given defining factor (e.g. time spent in each other's presence) constitutes an acceptable criterion. Other defining factors such as awareness of the presence of others and interaction, are equally important, but all are dependent for their existence upon the factor of time.

One zoologist (Jones 1967) has even suggested that the group state may be the real existence of which individuals are no more than parts, as cells are constituents of a body. Jones was in fact writing about social insects such as bees, but his argument is applicable to human beings, too. Thus, it is possible to argue that all social life is group life and that the individual is a more or less responsive constituent part.

Whyte (1960) proposes that we tend to be 'confusing an abstraction with a reality'. He goes on to say that because a collection of individuals can be called 'a group' it does not imply that they *function* as 'a group'. (This is an interesting example of the arbitrary way in which the term 'group' is used.) By saying that a collection of people does not function as a group, Whyte is suggesting that in his definition certain clear conditions must be present before the collection becomes a group. In his terms those conditions are those that facilitate a collection's ability to function as a group, that is, to act as an integrated unit with some cognizance of the interdependence of the constituent parts.

In general, I would not quarrel with this outlook. However, I do question the assumption that there is a *qualitative* difference between the 'collective' and the 'group'. As I see it, the difference is *quantitative*; the two systems are the same system at different stages in its development. All the factors that eventually create the group are in existence in the collectivity. They are less intensively and extensively developed, but they are there. Even this concept has an element of arbitrariness about it but I think it begs fewer questions, and is broader and more elegant than approaches that insist that the obvious differences between groups, crowds, and collectivities are differences of kind. No one would suggest that eggs, caterpillars, pupae, and moths are not part of the same life cycle despite their apparent differences.

Golembiewski (1962) asserts that he can find no evidence for the assumption that all human aggregates are groups. But it is equally clear from the definition he gives of a 'group' that once more he has made an arbitrary choice about what he will accept as falling within his criteria.

This leads to a search for the factors that distinguish what one will and will not accept under the rubric of 'group'. Hence all the concern with the awareness of purpose on the part of the members, the sense of belonging, and the myriad of focusing factors. In turn, this has led to semantic problems and to problems of infinite consequence in terms of the impossibility of comparing research projects ostensibly concerned with the same social situation, i.e. a group. Ultimately this has led to a hardening of the differences and possessive claims that only the writer is talking about 'real' groups.

Most particular and precise formulations about actual occurrences can be embedded in larger concepts and this stochastic process may be infinite. But there must be some stage at which the apparently separate theoretical entities can be embedded without harm or loss in the next larger stage of concept. If this is not done with the concept of group then the arbitrary nature remains paramount and conflict prevents maximum use being made of the available data.

WHAT ARE GROUPS?

'Our aim, therefore, is to enunciate general principles of the following form: "If any device is to perform function X, then that device is subject to or limited by the principles Y which must hold for all possible devices performing this function".'

(Miller 1969a : 107)

George Miller was writing about a way of comparing computers and human beings, machines and organisms, that sees them 'insofar as they performed the same function . . . as particular instances of theoretical systems of far greater generality' (Miller 1969a : 106).

The obvious difficulty of comparing groups which arises from the apparent widely different uses to which they are put, has always tended towards a differentiation of groups. The functions have been seen to be different. Therefore Miller's general principle would not apply. But it seems to me that 'function' in these instances is often confused with 'outcome'. For example, if a group is used as a method of treating people with particular kinds of emotional problems, then its outcome is therapeutic. Some would say that this was also its 'function' and that this function would be different from that of a group set up to enhance learning.

The point I want to make is that the functions of all groups, defined as the way they operate, are identical and that it is not so much the absolute difference of function that creates apparent difference in groups, but the intensity, duration, and selective use of the recognizably limited number of functions that produce different outcomes. In terms of Miller's general principles, all groups fit into a theoretical system of greater generality and are governed by the same general principles. In other words, these can be defined as a stochastic theory of groups that points to the similarities of groups rather than their differences.

Given a stochastic theory in which the different 'kinds' of groups (I would prefer to use the word 'manifestations' than 'kinds') can be embedded, we are immediately presented with the possibility of direct comparison of identifiable components. We are in fact faced with the possibility of examining the interactive behaviour of human beings in certain set pieces. The use of the word 'set' here indicates that the element of time has to be considered as one of the most important factors involved.

Human beings are separate entities but in their movements through space and time they gather together to produce groupings that last for different spans of time. Some like families and friendships, exist over long periods of time; others, like acquaintanceships or crowds, last only a short time. People also move from one of these gatherings to others in relatively short periods of time.

All this is very obvious but it has to be said because the collectivities themselves, especially if they are not particularly transient, have come to be regarded as entities so much in their own right that the obvious fact that they are collecting points in a never-ending stream of interaction tends to get lost, and with it the essential similarities that exist among them.

Shaw (1974) argues that group behaviour is the behaviour of the individuals who compose the group. Their behaviour in one group will be different from their solitary behaviour because the stimuli they receive from the presence of others are significantly different in different social situations. This is another way of asserting the same point I made earlier.

The constellations of individuals that a person enters are composed of different individuals and occur at different stages of the life cycle both of the individual members and of the gatherings they compose. Thus, the stimuli to which any one member is exposed are different – not in kind but in intensity and duration – and, indeed, perception of those stimuli also changes with experience and the degree of familiarity.

Once more, we are forced back to the fact that group behaviour is behaviour in the presence of others, the response to the ordinary stimuli of human social meeting. How long the gatherings stay together and thus increase the chance of adding to the experience of their members (which in turn modifies their perceptions not only of this collectivity but of all others of which they are a member) is crucial. Thus, although the terms 'natural' and 'created' groups are in widespread use to distinguish between what are often seen as the two major categories of grouping, it will be shown that the distinction relates only to the nature of their origin and not to the behaviour patterns of which they are composed.

So-called 'natural' groups

'If it were possible for the overworked hypothetical man from
Mars to take a fresh view of the people of Earth, he would
probably be impressed by the amount of time they spend doing
things in groups.'   (Cartwright and Zander 1953)

'Natural' groups tend to be those that were in existence long
before the person who so describes them saw them as such.
'Natural', in this sense, has little or nothing to do with nature but
with a sense of rightness, a feeling that such groups are 'real',
that they grew out of ordinary human needs and that there is no
immediate evidence that they were consciously and deliberately
brought into existence by one or more human beings as an act of
policy.

'Natural' also implies acceptance. The 'normal' state of affairs
has not been interfered with. People may not like families,
particularly their own, but a family is described as a 'natural'
group. It grows out of several very basic needs of all human
beings, all of which can only be met by some long-term contact
with, and support from, other people. It is real; it is accepted.

Employing the dichotomy of 'natural' / 'created' forms of
groups leads to the difficulty of actually seeing 'natural' groups
as groups. To many people the word 'group' means a collection of
individuals gathered together in one place at the same time often
for at least one common purpose. It is quite acceptable that a
study could be made of how such groups form, function, and die,
but it is quite another matter to want to apply similar techniques
to 'natural' groups such as families, friendship groups, and
gangs. This is one of the major reasons why information about
the ways in which groups behave is so heavily weighted in favour
of that obtained from 'artificial' groups (Argyle 1969).

There are other reasons, of course. For instance, the invasion
of an investigator into a 'natural' group throws into sharp relief
the fact that his or her reason for being there is significantly
different from that of all the other members. What the investigator sees may well be biased by the fact of his or her presence.
He or she can hardly ever become a true member of the group

unless their motives for being there change or are never made explicit.

Using Whyte's (1960) terminology, 'natural' groups would be called 'incidental' in contradistinction to 'created' groups, which would be called 'functional'. So Whyte's distinction lies in whether a group form arose to meet or accommodate the exigencies of an 'in-process' situation and in that sense is a spontaneous growth from that situation, or whether a conscious effort is directed to the establishment of a group form 'designed' to cope with a situation and to facilitate a predicated outcome.

A somewhat similar formulation is put forward by Heap (1977) in which the factors of spontaneity, chance, propinquity, shared interests, and needs are regarded as prime elements in the gestation of 'natural' groups. There is strong emphasis on the chance element of people being in the same place at the same time and a sense of the benefits this brings that reinforces the desire to maintain the source. (Heap uses the phrase 'members simply come together'.)

It is precisely this chance element and the desire to maintain a group as a source of satisfaction that offers the possibility of discovering what factors in these groups, when they endure, meet the needs of their members so well. In other words, if a grouping arises from the chance factors listed above, stays in existence for a considerable period of time, and creates behaviour patterns that can not only be recognized but emulated, then that group effectively serves the needs of its members. Moreover, the shape or form it has developed should be the embodiment of the elements that generate effective need-satisfaction in this kind of situation. In a sense it is 'organic' in that it has grown into the shape it finally assumes.

To be more sure of this point it is necessary to look at groups that do not originate in this way and to identify the major differences and the likely effects.

So-called 'created' groups

'the group is artificial, a form created by design'

'1   Artificial things are synthesized (though not always or usually with full forethought) by man.

2   Artificial things may imitate appearances in natural things while lacking, in one or more respects, the reality of the latter.

3   Artificial things can be characterised in terms of functions, goals, adaptations.

4   Artificial things are often discussed, particularly when they are being designed, in terms of imperatives as well as descriptives.'   (Simon in Rosenthal 1973 : 61)

One major problem in the world of groups is that of gaining acceptance for the idea of the similarity of all groups. The terms 'natural' and 'created' groups embody this problem. There is something alien about groups that are created as a specific effort of will. In teaching people to see the dynamics of groups, for instance, a very common comment is that any group studied for this purpose is 'artificial'. By this is meant that a very strong resistance to the group's 'realness' has been generated, despite the fact that the group is constituted of real people in real surroundings. The element of being conscious of its generation and purpose, of being in on its birth rather than just finding it already in existence, seems to cause problems in accepting its reality.

The major distinctions between 'natural' and 'created' groups would seem to be first that natural groups arise out of the everyday needs of human beings (they are of spontaneous generation and arise from circumstances that occur as an integral part of human existence) and, second, that for the individual member the sense of 'naturalness' is greater the further away he or she is from the actual creation of the group.

In a very arbitrary way the terms 'natural' and 'created' groups define not so much different kinds of animal but different ways of looking at members of the same species. The use of the word 'natural' gives the clue to the kind of thinking that lies behind it as does the use of the word 'artificial' for groups that are specifically and consciously generated. Matters have often been made worse by attempts to prove what happens in all groups by creating experimental groups and performing controlled experiments with carefully delineated areas of group behaviour. This lays open the possibility of direct refusal to accept any results from such groups, which are quite rightly seen as artificial, to 'real' groups, which by definition are natural.

There is a problem with experimental group data but it is not their absolute distinction from real groups. It is the fact that experimental groups are created for the purpose of being experimental groups – their purpose is to perform an experimental function. Thus, all the factors that attend their creation, function, constitution, and performance, affect the outcome. To transfer an analysis of such outcomes directly to the understanding of groups where the factors are different in some major way is not to be wholly wrong (that would contravene the essential similarity of all groups), but to have an instrument that is woefully out of balance.

The question of the 'created' group and its difference is not one of kind but of quantity and quality of the major influencing factors. Looked at in this way, it is possible to say that the so-called 'natural' group has some considerable elements of 'artificiality' in it, that is, elements deliberately brought into existence or modified in some way by conscious effort, but that mainly its structure has come about by 'chance' elements.

A large number of so-called 'natural' groups are transient by nature. They come into being to meet a given situation and break up when that situation no longer obtains. It is only when the group deliberately seeks other similar situations to work at, becomes consciously interested in its own performance, and deliberately attempts to improve its methods, that the group has begun to move from its chance origin to a rationally constructed performing unit. This kind of change concerns time and the changed perceptions of members about their achievement, satisfactions, and functions.

Processes take some time to become established and to produce outcomes, and so although the so-called 'natural' groups should give us clear indications of the factors that allow the group to stay in business, not all 'natural' groups are germane to our purpose. Essentially the natural groups that should prove most valuable in providing the evidence required should not be transient and should be successful in the performance of their function. For these reasons I have chosen to look at groups that have a permanence beyond one initial function. It is their successful forms that I want to scrutinize. Groups modify their members' experience of group behaviour and this modification, or learning process, is often referred to as the 'influence' that a group can exert.

THE NATURE OF GROUP INFLUENCE

'a great deal of behaviour which has been supposed to emanate from within the individual, to be based on his fixed character traits, is, in fact, a function of the individual within his group.'

(Brown 1954 : 283)

'Influence is neither good nor bad in an absolute manner, but only in relation to the one who experiences it.'   (Gide 1903)

Without doubt, groups possess the ability to influence the behaviour of their members. Indeed, it is the nature of this ability, and the methods employed that are fundamental to this study. If a group is not able by its very nature to influence its members and to moderate their behaviour, then any attempt to use a group for this kind of purpose is certain to fail.

First we must clarify what is meant by influence, looking at group influence in general terms here but in more detail in the subsequent sections. To begin with, it is necessary to recognize the two most important elements, that is, the actual influence or pressure that a group exerts and the perception that each member has of the pressure being exerted. The necessity to behave in specific acceptable ways can be spelled out clearly by the group through its representatives, or it can be left to be discovered by newly acquired members who are helped by hint, suggestion, modelling, and sanction. In any case, each member's perception of what the group requires of him or her will be somewhat idiosyncratic. The possibility for error and partial success is enormous and tends to increase, the more specific the required behaviours become.

One fact, substantially backed by practical experience, emerges fairly clearly from a consideration of the material about group influence. This concerns the relationship between influence, the need for a particular group, and the availability of alternative groups. Given that a group must satisfy some of the needs of its members better, in their opinion, than any available alternatives, there must come a point where any increase in the demands of a group on its members could make previously unattractive substitutes a better base of satisfaction. Thus, if freedom to change exists, change will take place. Group influence can only operate as an acceptable pressure up to the point at which the satisfactions derived from being a member of the group are greater than the dissatisfactions generated by the group pressure. If alternatives or substitutes are available then the 'cost' rate may well tilt in their favour and if the pressure is great enough then opting out altogether may become viable.

Thus, the nature of group influence can be described in terms of an exchange. In so far as any group meets the needs of an individual, the costs will be the demands the group makes on that individual. If, in the opinion of the individual, the costs exceed the rewards, alternative and cheaper ways of meeting needs will be sought. As the needs of human beings are many and varied, it must suffice to say that the most basic needs reside in the constant requirements for reassurance of the accepting presence of others, confirmation of our existence, and the dispelling of fear of rejection and isolation. As human contact is an essential ingredient in all these needs, then a group must be an ideal medium for meeting them.

While easy to talk about, the concept of satisfaction is actually almost impossible to define. Often enough in any situation there are many hidden satisfactions and many hidden costs that can only be guessed at as motivators of individual behaviour. Furthermore, the apparently increasing value offered by alternatives is of no consequence in determining action if they are not perceived as substitutes. This may be either because the individual has never realized the existence of, or potential value of the alternatives, or because the information about them leads to an incorrect assessment of their value.

There are situations where no substitutes exist and where physical withdrawal is not possible either. Similarly, there are situations where one group constitutes the sole possible source of satisfaction of needs for its members. In both cases the amount of influence that the group can exert is almost infinite. However, in the former it is likely to be countered by forms of psychological withdrawal, while in the latter it may well be accepted, whatever the personal cost, because the alternatives – absolute isolation or death – are not often preferable. These extremes are mentioned because most of us are members of many groups. Our needs are diffused and met through a spectrum of memberships and often the influence of any one group can never increase to intolerable levels because there are too many viable alternatives available.

Group pressure is exerted upon individuals through the group's perceived ability to meet the needs of these individuals. The nature, extent, and intensity of those needs form the upward limits of the pressure that a group can exert. It is so important that we need to look at it in some more explicit detail. And, as one of the major elements of group influence is pressure towards conformity, then this factor needs to be looked at.

Conformity

'Conformity can be defined as a change in a person's behaviour or opinions as a result of real or imagined pressures from a person or group of people.'   (Aronson 1976 : 17)

'the action of a subject when he goes along with his peers, people of his own status, who have no special right to direct his behaviour.'   (Milgram 1974 : 113)

'a conformist might be defined as a person who has managed to avoid being defined as a deviant.'   (Schur 1979 : 18)

From the foregoing it must be clear that in group influence we are talking about a group's ability as a unit to control, at least at the public presentation level, the behaviour of its members in all or some selected areas of their behaviour. This is behaviour in conformity with the generally accepted norms of the group. In all group situations members have perceptions of the nature of the sanctions that the group can apply for behaviour that contravenes those norms. Only in very few groups are sanctions the same for all members and the behaviour that will entail sanctions is related to the member's status.

Response to conformity pressures varies according to many different factors. While the more intelligent group members are less likely to conform, authoritarian personalities are more likely to do so. Where the membership of a group contains both sexes, conformity levels are higher than in single-sex groups. Other variables that relate to increasing conformity are the size of the majority in favour, the ambiguity of the situation, agreement among most other members, and the open and decentralized nature of the group's communication systems (Shaw 1974:).

If a member sees that most of the other members are more competent than he or she is, then he or she is much more likely to conform to the pressures that the group exerts. Conformity is related to security and acceptance, the sense of not being alone in having to face the problems of life, and it induces order into the group situation with the enhanced probability of integrating and co-ordinating individual behaviour.

Aronson (1976) suggests that in unfamiliar situations we tend to conform to the behaviour of others whom we suspect 'know the ropes'. Aronson asserts that the behaviour we learn in this way tends to be enduring because it is an exercise in determining reality, an attempt to make sense of a part of our world that, being unfamiliar, lacks security.

Fear lies at the base of conformity, the fear of not being accepted. The greater the respect an individual has for the others of his group members, the more need there is to be accepted, and the greater is the pressure that the group can exert to produce a public conformity to its norms, rules, and standards. But public conformity is not necessarily private acceptance and it is this (a continuing conformity even when the pressure to conform is removed) that is the element of change. This will be taken up in more detail in the next section.

Festinger's (1957) concept of cognitive dissonance helps to explain something of conformity pressure. The tension created by holding conflicting cognitions has to be resolved by first, changing one element of the behaviour; second, finding examples that reduce its dissonant effect; or third, creating cognitions that indicate that the dissonant behaviour is in fact good and beneficial. The reduction of an individual's dissatisfaction in a social situation is achieved by producing behaviour acceptable to the others or by redefining needs relative to the situation.

If there are alternative sources of need satisfaction available, for example, other groups, then, if there are no restrictions on movement, when the pressure to conform becomes too great it will tend to reduce an individual's level of satisfaction for his or her group below the point where these alternative sources become more attractive. When this happens, the individual will move, for even the dissatisfactions and consequences of moving can be overcome if the pressure is great enough. This is a serious consideration for groups where members cannot move and where pressure generating high levels of dissatisfaction exists. Psychological withdrawal may be one method of coping, but others, much more disruptive and designed to change the situation, are equally likely.

Allen (1965) suggested that apart from the problem of private and public acceptance there are ten situational factors that influence an individual's response to group conformity pressures:

1 The level of commitment to the group.
2 The level of attractiveness of the group.
3 Status in the group.
4 The degree of interdependence within the group.
5 The group's composition.
6 The group's size and unanimity.
7 The extent to which the nature of the group norms are extreme.
8 Whether the group is task competent.

9   What level of task-confidence exists.
10   How difficult and important the task is.

Allen ended his essay on situational factors in conformity thus:
'Neither should we fail to realize that other modes of response to
group pressure are available to a person in addition to conformity
or nonconformity' (Allen 1965 : 142). Conformity is dependent
behaviour. It requires that those it affects should be of equal
status. It spreads by imitation. The requirement to conform is
implicit and the conformist believes that his or her autonomy has
been retained. Tactical conformity may be an ingratiating act but
in general conformity means 'bringing one's behaviour within
bounds defined as acceptable by group members and doing one's
best to meet their expectations' (Sherif 1976 : 100). It is a democratic process in that it attempts to create sameness.

Compliance

'This term best describes the mode of behaviour of a person
who is motivated by a desire to gain reward or avoid punishment. Typically his behaviour is only as long-lived as is the
promise of the reward or the threat of punishment.'

(Aronson 1976 : 29)

'He that complies against his will [i]s of his own opinions still.'
(Butler 1663 : 33)

Compliance is another possible response to the influence a group
can exert. A consideration of compliance brings into focus the
problems of public and private behaviour. On the face of it,
compliance appears to be conformity. The compliant person
apparently accepts the norms, standards, and values of the
system he or she is currently inhabiting. His or her reasons for
this behaviour are obvious. Like an animal that blends with its
background, the compliant person becomes unnoticed and
acceptable. In a word, he or she has ensured personal security,
freedom to move about, and an avoidance of being highlighted as
being different.

The newcomer to an established group encounters problems
precisely of this nature. If there is a strong need to belong and to

be accepted, then there will be compliance with the demands made by the group without any realization of the real reasons for these demands. When the individual feels secure, he or she may not only be able to question or even resist some of the demands, but also be able to assess the consequences of such non-compliance upon his or her satisfaction. Compliance equates obedience and appears to arise as an attempt on the part of an individual to attract reward and avoid punishment. The behaviour tends to last only as long as the promise of reward or threat is sustained as behaviour can change when the situation changes. However, there is some indication that compliance with small demands facilitates compliance with larger requests, probably because the complying person has already become involved and also because his or her attitudes may have been significantly changed by the first act of compliance.

The basic factor in compliance is the compliant person's perception of the ability of the influencer to give rewards or punishments. This equates with the first of five social powers delineated by French and Raven (1959). If the power referent is constantly in attendance then compliant behaviour assumes a greater durability. Similarly, if the compliant person's satisfactions are increased by the act of compliance either in the actions themselves or the consequences of those actions then the compliant state will tend to endure.

Generally speaking, the compliant person holds complying opinions and values lightly and does not believe in them. He or she is demonstrating a public compliance. Milgram (1974) believed that the reward received by the compliant person may be a 'profound emotional gratification' and suggested that compliant behaviour took place in a hierarchical structure; it was not imitative, its prescriptions were explicit, and compliant people tended to resign their autonomy.

Compliance perpetuates inequality and is concerned with the maintenance of differentials. But from the point of view of the compliant person it is one way of dealing with social influence; it provides security and a breathing space without undue commitment.

Identification

Identification is another response to group pressure. To identify indicates a desire to be like the influencer and is concerned with attractiveness. Satisfaction in this case resides in taking on the values, opinions, and beliefs of the influencer, and creating a self-denying relationship. Negative identification is possible in which dislike engenders rejection of all that the disliked influencer stands for.

Identification appears to be a very powerful agent in advertising and selling because people whom the advertising audience like, and can identify with, can influence opinion about products as long as these are not too important. Similarly, prejudices can be picked up by identification with people who hold them.

The continuous pressure necessary in compliance is not essential in identification, which is associated with, and conterminous with, the perception of the source of influence. This can be seen as three important variables:

1   The influencer needs to remain important.
2   The influencer needs to continue to hold the same beliefs.
3   The identifier's beliefs are not challenged by opinions that turn out to be logically more convincing.

The latter shows that identification contains as part of the satisfaction to the identifier a large element of the desire to be right.

Internalization

Conformity, compliance, and identification are relatively transient responses to group pressure, internalization is not. As with identification, there is a strong element of the desire to be right in its formation. The satisfaction that internalization gives is thus intense and this allows the influence to become independent of the source and an integral part of the internalizer.

If the influencing agent, group, or person is perceived as trustworthy and as possessing good judgement, then the values and beliefs of that agent will become an integral part of the internalizer's value system. They will become his or her values and will be very difficult to change. As the desire to be right (that is, not to appear to be stupid, ignorant, or foolish) is a very powerful and self-sustaining motivation, the continued presence of the influencing agent is not necessary and may even be forgotten after a period of time.

Because of these factors the internalizer has more flexible responses than is allowed by any of the other responses because the system he or she is operating from is his or her private system based on credibility.

Reference and membership groups

'In social psychological theory, it has long been recognized that an individual's *membership groups* have an important influence on the values and attitudes he holds. More recently, attention has also been given to the influence of his *reference groups*: the groups in which he aspires to attain or maintain membership.'   (Siegel and Siegel 1957 : 300)

Although reference groups will be considered again later, it is appropriate to discuss them briefly here under the context of group influence. Reference groups have been called 'invisible committees' and appear to act as a standard against which an individual measures his or her performance. Even the knowledge that he or she may never actually come face to face with one of his or her reference groups – indeed, it may no longer be in existence like the childhood family – does not appear to lessen the influence its norms can have on behaviour. A degree of internalization of the standards and values of the reference group has taken place so that these values become integrated in the individual and need no continuing support from the source. It is this particular influence on an individual's action that is so hard to appreciate.

Carolyn Sherif (1976) calls reference groups and persons 'the social connections of self' and illustrates the point by showing how the many groups of which she is, and has been, a member are her 'social anchors', the links that tie her to the society in which she lives and which in large measure give meaning to her life. In any one social situation most of these 'social anchors' are not visible, but they can have quite a great effect on the behaviour of the anchored individual. How can an observer interpret behaviour that is not wholly related to the current observable scene but partly to a hidden and powerful pre-programming?

The greater the individual's respect for his or her reference group, the more he or she will have internalized their norms. These will become the standards to live by, guides to relationships, and will establish attitudes and condition responses to major life events. Not all of the individual's reference groups will fit happily together and there may well be conflicting messages.

Some reference groups and persons may not be human or real in the sense that they can be fictional, historical, or imaginary. What is important is that they represent and produce standards that can be integrated into an individual's value scheme. It is possible to stretch the concept to include ideas, abstract principles, and ideals as forming standards in the same way. As Sprott (1958 : 60) has said, 'We are to a large measure the artefacts of our affiliations'.

Two other responses need to be given brief consideration. These are co-operation and competition.

Co-operation

Because co-operative behaviour (that is, going along with others) has great survival value, it is a response to group pressure that is well understood by most people. It is dependent on the perception that in order to achieve a given goal individuals need one another. If the goal is important (i.e. superordinate), then individuals will be willing to sacrifice other important personal issues in order to co-operate with others in its attainment. While co-operative endeavour is in progress, a state of mutual interdependence occurs and there is a tendency to reduce hostility and prejudice and to increase friendliness and attentiveness to others.

Competition

Competition is formed strongly on the need to achieve and seems to be an essential element of Western society. Aggressive behaviour, the need to dominate, to succeed, and to do well are all aspects of competition between individuals and groups. Pre-judice, discrimination, and stereotyping are all strengthened in the presence of competition.

THE NATURE OF CONSTRAINTS

'It becomes necessary to see any group, artificial or natural, as existing within a milieu which places upon the group limita-tions and boundaries.'   (Douglas 1979 : 78)

In the analysis of what goes on in groups, it is often forgotten that the object of analysis exists in relation to a myriad surroundings. This forgetfulness can promote neglect and ignorance of the effects that these surrounding factors can have. One of the possible reasons may be the difficulty of defining what these constraining influences are and isolating and measuring their effects. Nevertheless, to acknowledge their presence is a step in the right direction no matter how crude the defining entities may be.

A second problem relating to constraints is that once more we are dealing not with a direct cause/effect situation but one that is monitored and modified by the nature of individual perception and response. For instance, the passing of time is a fact. The way it affects members of a group depends largely how each perceives the time factor in relation to their own needs and priorities.

While this perceptual factor complicates the assessment of the way in which existing constraints affect the influence processes in a group, all outcomes in group situations are influenced by them because the nature of constraint is present in every consti-tuent factor of the group and its surroundings. It needs to be said here that the term 'constraint' may be misleading in that it appears to have a restrictive connotation. While this is true, the positive side is the security that a defining structure, boundary, or limit can give. I have found that the most useful way of thinking about the constraints is that when they are recognized and their constraining function assessed in relation to the par-ticular group under consideration, they define what is possible.

This way of looking at constraints has then to have an extra dimension, summed up in the dichotomy modifiable/non-modifiable. Modifiable, that is, from the point of view of the group (in reality whether the group possesses the power to effect change). Constraints that are non-modifiable immediately set the parameters within which the group can function, while admitting that the assessment of their nature as unmodifiable may be incorrect and prove to be so at some later stage.

Second and third factors enter into this debate under the rubrics of duration and intensity. In the first case (duration), constraints that at one point in time are assessed as non-modifiable may not continue their existence in that form for the duration of the group's existence. Factors totally separate from the group and its immediate milieu can materially affect the operating constraints (administrative decisions, changes in the power structure, and financial change, for example). These changes can obviously work in either direction, tightening or loosening the constraints' effect.

The third factor (intensity) is inherent in the factor of change also. Some constraints have little effect upon a group despite being non-modifiable, others have a great deal. This level of intensity of effect can, of course, change during the life of a group either from the effect of outside influence or from a change in the group's need of, or response to, the constraint in question. What matters is that all constraints are constantly monitored in order to assess the effects they are producing.

A list of the constraints is given in Douglas (1979 : 78–106) where a discussion of their nature is pursued at some length. In one sense everything that comprises a group and the milieu in which it is embedded can have some effect on its outcome. Group members clearly react to things as intangible as the atmosphere of the place where they meet just as much as they may do to the constrictions of material resources, such as space, equipment, and finance. So it is only realistic that the recognition and assessment of constraints, and the continuous monitoring of their effect, should be restricted to those that are considered to create the most important positive and negative effects.

As I hope to show later, groups that have arisen to meet specific ends and that assume a traditional form, take on this structure and design largely, though not wholly, because experience has shown which constraints have the power to affect outcomes and which design elements can enhance, use, or reduce those effects to the benefit of the group. It becomes important, therefore, not only to recognize these traditional, empirically developed structures for the design elements they are, but also to be aware of constraints that are not part of the basic traditional pattern but which are present in a current situation in which it is proposed to embed a group.

Apart from the environment and the element of time, which I mentioned earlier, the acts of leadership, made by group members, form a very large part of a group's constraint system. The element of choice, which is a characteristic of leadership acts, is always selective. Thus, choosing to go in one direction and to behave according to this norm always constrains the group, if the choice is accepted, by cutting off the possibility of doing something else.

Leadership acts as a specific form of constraint

'No man is great enough or wise enough for any of us to surrender our destiny to. The only way in which any one can lead us is to restore to us the belief in our own guidance.'

(Miller 1941)

The issue of leadership has always been one of the major areas of debate in the study of groups. The concepts of democracy and equality have tended to produce a suspicion of the exercise of power and to inhibit the movement of individuals into leadership roles. Theories of leadership have tended to be concerned with the kind of people who make good leaders or with the kind of situations that pushed people into being a leader. The difference between a public profession of leadership as autocratic and undemocratic, and the private ambitions to power and dominion over others are well noted in our society.

But members of a group do seek to achieve something from their membership and there is never any guarantee that the group will provide even the bare minimum of satisfaction for the individual without some guidance from him or her of the way he or she would wish it to go. Of course the dissatisfaction to be incurred by attempting to change the rewards produced by group membership in line with increasing them may balance out or even be too great so that greater actual reward can accrue to the individual by not interfering with the status quo. Even this situation can be shown to carry with it some aspect of a leadership act in that a decision not to intervene in the group process does affect the outcome; it produces an apparent agreement with the current movement that can enhance the belief of other members that the group is fulfilling its purpose.

Leadership acts are defined as those behaviours taken by group members that influence or attempt to influence the process of the group. Decisions not to do something are just as important in this respect as decisions that lead to more positive action. But the characteristic of all leadership acts that brings them into the category of constraint is the element of choice. In considering the positive nature of choosing to do A, it is often forgotten that one has equally positively chosen not to do B, or C, or Z! In this sense, given a range of possible actions or non-actions, a leadership act is a choice that one or more of the available actions is preferable and, if this leadership act is effective (that is, it causes this choice to be accepted), then the group has been constrained to move in a particular way at that particular time.

The nature of leadership acts is that they are based upon the perception of an individual that something needs to be done. There may be a wide range of motivations for that perception, ranging all the way from ensuring personal security to a clear perception of the group's needs as a unit to be influenced to move in a particular direction in line with its accepted purpose. Clearly such a perception, while a necessary prerequisite of action, is not by itself a sufficient reason for taking it. The individual also has to have perceptions about his or her ability to take that action, to assess the cost he or she envisages might be incurred, and to decide whether it will be successful or not (that is, whether it is worth the risk involved).

In all these perceptions there is the chance that they do not, and will not, coincide with the way others see the situation. Thus, one basic risk is always present in any leadership act, that is, the individual's perception is idiosyncratic and may not be congruent with the perception of others. His or her individual perception may be more prescient than theirs, but many factors (status, for example) might be involved in any attempt to convince. There are many instances of individuals 'going along' with decisions against their better judgement, often for reasons of personal security, and where subsequent events have demonstrated the correctness or appropriateness of their withheld perception (see, for example, Steiner 1974; Torrance 1954; Kelman 1950; and Hochbaum 1954).

Whatever the origin of leadership acts, whether from desig-nated leader or not, their nature is influential and their effect constraining. Such acts can be directed to many parts of group behaviour, to all the group processes, to individuals, to sub-groups, to the whole group, and to the constraints both within and without. They can be aimed at the task performance of the group or at its internal or external relationships, to factors external to the group that affect its outcomes, and so on – the list is endless.

Given that leadership is such an important constraining factor, the way it is built into the design of any group will have far-reaching consequences for the degree of success or failure that group will have in achieving its proximate and long-range goals.

SUMMARY

This chapter has been concerned to describe some of the basic nature of human groups and to look at the factor of prime importance, influence. It has been argued that all groupings, ranging from what might be called 'chaotic aggregates' through to clearly defined 'systems' that are stable and enduring, have a large number of basic similarities. The behavioural patterns that emerge are identical but at different levels of intensity and are certainly susceptible to different degrees of conscious control.

Some groups are regarded as 'natural', that is, arising more or less spontaneously out of need, or 'created', that is, specifically designed to meet some need. All groups are influence systems and the pressure they can generate was looked at under the rubrics of conformity, compliance, identification, and internalization. Equally, all groups are subject to constraints, the nature of which was discussed; leadership acts, a prime constraint, was singled out for more detailed analysis.

3

GROUP PROCESSES

INTRODUCTION

'It is indisputable that our universe is not chaos. We perceive beings, objects, things to which we give names. These beings or things are forms or structures endowed with a degree of stability, they take up some part of space and last for some period of time.' (Thom in Postle 1980 : 29)

In writing about the nature of groups, psychologists and group workers of all kinds have tended to talk about 'group processes'. Groups, being dynamic entities, must have processes, that is, chains of events with a beginning, middle, and end sequentially linked. But although it is one thing to say this, and another to know that such processes exist from experience, it is much more complex to define and distinguish these events. Most writers mention one or more group processes, and few define even those they mention clearly. However, all accept that some understanding of group processes is essential in any analysis of what happens in group situations.

Here we are faced with a very old dilemma. Do group processes actually exist as entities in their own right or are the words we use about the functions we call 'group processes' merely imposed names, labels that help us to make some sense of what appears to be happening? I am not sure that an answer to this question is very relevant. A considerable amount of psychological theory is abstract in that it relates to ways of formalizing and systematizing thoughts, it is not dealing with concrete quantifiable factors. What does matter is that the analysis of group processes should lead to the development of an increased understanding of group functioning and to the development of techniques for modifying it deliberately and purposefully based on that understanding.

In essence, whatever the nature of group processes, any analysis of them should be usable. The main reason for requiring explanations of why things happen must be to gain assurance that some measure of control (in terms of understanding and of response to such happenings) is possible in the future. From the start, then, it is irrelevant whether these so-called 'processes' are artificial in the sense that they are descriptive labels. What does matter is that it can be demonstrated that their use actually facilitates our understanding of the complex multi-dimensional dynamics of a group in action.

It is interesting in this respect to find that people who work with, and write about, groups seem often to be describing similar things. There are at least two reasons why this might be. First, they are looking at the same things, i.e. processes. Second, because of a similar background and a shared vocabulary, they are imposing the same interpretive labels on what are possibly discrepant events. A third approach might be to say that all such descriptions have elements of both sources in them.

However, the main purposes of describing anything are to make possible recognition of future occurrences and to make experience of such occurrences indirectly available to others. In a word, to create instruments whereby events not previously experienced become recognizable and their nature and possible consequences become known. Most importantly this confers the possibility of action to support, enhance, deflect, change, or eradicate those consequences, that is, a calculated response based upon knowledge and not a response that is at best a chance event.

In this process of the development of probable control we must not lose sight of another fact that arises from the use of such instruments, which is the post hoc analysis that reveals why certain events occurred and why they took the paths that were actually followed. In order to do this the instruments do not need

to be very precisely refined. Indeed, the concept of group processes is fairly crude. The described processes are not orthogonal;
indeed, some are remarkably vague, expressing very widespread
and accepted ideas that are yet very amorphous. Yet they provide
an instrument of analysis that is applicable to all forms of human
collectivity and is therefore a basis for logical comparisons.

THE IDENTIFICATION OF GROUP PROCESSES

'The selection of facts demands some way of determining
relevance.'   (Russell in de Maré 1972 : 85)

Perhaps the most efficient method of identifying group processes
is that of analysing what descriptive material exists, looking for
points of similarity and difference. Different witnesses may well
give different labels to similar things, but their descriptions
should, by the collation of similarities, quite quickly expose such
naming problems. Descriptions may be made at many different
levels, may cover vastly different areas of a situation, be parts
rather than wholes, and be subjectively determined by strongly
held beliefs about what should exist. Most of these problems are
familiar enough to students of the skills of observation.

I have already carried out the work of collating the material
available about group processes and extracting from it what
seemed to be the smallest number of described sequential patterns compatible with covering the whole ground (Douglas
1979). But further investigation and use of the ten items I
isolated requires further comment.

It has been customary to analyse what goes on in a group in
terms of the individual relationships that are produced within it.
This is natural enough. In psychology there has always been a
very strong emphasis on the individual and, until recently, an
almost equal lack of consideration of the effect of the individual's
social milieu. Individual psychologies were paramount when the
early investigations with group behaviour began. It was inevitable that the instruments of analysis that were readily available
should have been used. Much valuable work arose from this
situation and it still forms a basic layer of possible understand-

ing. However, what soon presented itself was the possibility of a different kind of understanding related not so much to individual interaction but to the patterns of behaviour of the group as unit.

Over time, the individual interactions of members performed within the context and boundary of the group produce outcomes for the group as a whole. Probably the first perception of patterns of this nature related to the observation that the historical sequence of group life showed a developmental pattern that was often likened to the maturational process of the human infant. In like manner, this maturational or developmental pattern was often represented as occurring in stages and there was a growing realization that these stages carried with them significantly different potentialities for the group as a whole. Of course, the patterns were, and are, too simple even when they stopped being linear and became cyclic, spiral, or regressive. But they demonstrated that it was possible to define a process larger than individual interactions because it was composed of a number of them executed over a period of time.

Other patterns could be discovered that were also mainly located in incidents that occurred in groups with sufficient frequency to become first expected and later predictable. Social structure was one such pattern, the ways a group developed to handle the making of decisions was another. A secondary level of analysis was now possible that related directly to time and the successful performance of the group tasks. This in turn gave the possibility of influencing such group outcomes by inhibiting the processes that might be counterproductive and, equally, by promoting those that moved the group towards achievement. In other words, it gave the possibility of a larger approach to the understanding and control of group behaviour.

Of course, these large patterns are formed by constellations of different kinds of individual interaction that thus form the basic and universal component of all the patterns. Indeed, the methods of influencing the larger patterns often lies in intervention in significant individual interactions that in turn modify the larger patterns that develop from them.

In effect, therefore, the identification of individual group processes constitutes a recognition of those patterns that are sufficiently different to warrant a separate existence. Often enough this identification has been made by group practitioners without full understanding of what they are describing and the terminology used to describe them does not always facilitate recognition and easy categorization.

However, there is more than ample evidence that those who work with groups can and do recognize behaviours that cluster in particular ways not only in terms of the nature of such behaviours, but in the frequency of their occurrence and their intensity, and in their spread or diffusion through the group, which, in time, actually create either a structure, a movement, or some more amorphous though readily recognizable ambience. It is these creations and the means by which they are created and maintained that form the group processes and that I take as the central theme of this book.

The non-orthogonal nature of group processes

The descriptive nature of the information on which identification is based, must of necessity lead to many similar factors being included in each of the apparently discrete elements defined. This may cause some confusion but it is not necessarily a stumbling block. For instance, it is possible to say that unless the members of a group interact with each other then not only is there no group but there are no group processes either. This does not mean that there is no point in looking beyond interaction to establish an understanding of group behaviour, nor that interaction is all that such behaviour comprises. It does mean that interaction is a fundamental process and as such is a constituent or generative factor in all other processes that may be discerned.

One way of describing the group processes is to say that they are not orthogonal. They overlap; parts of some are identical to parts of others – they are not mutually exclusive. In short, we are able to identify clearly the peaks of mountains in a range that at some lower and more basic level are interconnected. This is not a good analogy because mountain ranges are fixed and what one sees in a group in action is fluid and dynamic. A better analogy might be a large area of fluid where the shapes of waves are recognizable but where each wave is just as likely to be composed of a large part of fluid we have seen in another wave form a few moments ago as to be completely new material.

The most important features of recognition here are founded first in past experience, and, second, in frequency of occurrence.

Past experience All groups show striking similarities that are recognizable by people who have never heard of group processes or group dynamics. What they recognize is behaviour that has a degree of familiarity; it has a pattern. The pattern is not precisely the same (it could not be) but it is sufficiently similar to spark off recognition.

Frequency of occurrence In dynamic situations any sense of structure, of component parts, is established on the basis of patterns forming in roughly the same way. The constituents coalesce, break, and re-form but with sufficient frequency to develop an expectation that a given situation will generate a given pattern. This has at least two major implications.

First, prediction: recognition of a situation associated with the usual development of a given pattern will spark off an expectation that such a pattern will develop. This is the element of prediction and therefore looks to the future. Second, the past: if a pattern develops then it is more likely that it arose from a particular constellation of events that, from past experience, one knows produce this form. Even though this constellation was not actually witnessed, its existence can be predicated on the basis of what followed it, in much the same way that the one-time existence of galactic bodies can be asserted from the patterns of disturbance they created although the original body is no longer a concrete reality.

What this amounts to is that group processes are not exact. It is not possible to use them to quantify the dynamics of a group with mathematical precision. In effect, precision of that nature would be valueless. Even counting the number of times a given interaction behaviour takes place over a period of time adds little of value to a group operator's understanding when he or she already has some idea of the frequency of such a behaviour pattern in terms of many or few interactions.

'Historically one of the main arguments for the study of groups has been that groups are not mere summations of individuals but a different system level, with properties arising from the pattern of member characteristics in interaction with the situation.'   (McGrath and Altman 1966 : 60)

The problem of describing group processes is highlighted by Collins and Guetzkow (1964) in *Social Psychology of Group Processes for Decision-making*. There are the words 'Group Processes' in the title and there are several references throughout the text to the major part such processes play, for example, 'But the extensive data contrasting an individual working alone with the same individual working in a group give us an insight into the unique properties of group processes' (1964 : 10). This is an excellent way of assessing the impact of group processes, but these processes are never defined. There is no reference to them as such in the otherwise very comprehensive index. Is the assumption that group processes are so obvious that no one needs even to be reminded what they are?

But the same neglect is true of most other texts. No matter whether one looks for the processes under the heading of group dynamics or elsewhere, the basic assumption seems to be that such commonly known factors only require to be mentioned for us to know precisely what is meant. We are left with the basic tasks of defining first what is meant by a group process and, second, trying to isolate as many group processes as possible.

The lexical definition of a process combines the notions of action, operation, or change, natural or involuntary, that occur over a period of time. A problem immediately arises when we try to talk about the processes that occur in a group – in fact not one but several problems occur. First, and importantly, human groups cannot be regarded as amalgams of constituents that affect one another in prescribed ways, as for instance occurs in the combination or mixture of chemical substances. Human beings are conscious of their involvement and can rationally (or otherwise) take action based upon their perception of what is happening to modify it. How can we say, therefore, that the people who compose a group at some stage become the constituents of that group which then can be analysed in terms of the processes it (that is, the group) produces?

The main evidence that can be adduced for following this apparently ambiguous procedure is historical. Even taking into account the psychological or other orientation of the observer, which inevitably would introduce some element of seeing what he or she expected to see, people who observe groups have recorded remarkable similarities in the way they behave. Thus, historically we find descriptions of group behaviour in terms of individual interaction in the presence of others turning to statements of the linear sequence a group pursues during its life, to cyclic sequences and spirals, through to the presentation of observable patterns that relate to the group as an identifiable entity and not to the behaviour as individuals of its constituent members.

There are no clearly defined edges to these patterns and some are more easily and readily identifiable than others, but the fact remains that they can be noticed. If they relate to the group as an existing entity, then attempts to change, support, or modify the group should prove much more effective when directed at the group's own patterns than when directed solely at the behaviour of its constituent members.

For the purposes of this book I would like to use the patterns I have previously identified (Douglas 1979) as a working base and give them here in simple form (*Table 1*).

I have previously always regarded group processes as a function of interaction but it is obviously possible to see the prime factor in their generation as lying elsewhere. This being so, it is now necessary to look briefly at the assumption that interaction is the prime generative factor, and, second, at the value of using group influence or communication to fulfil that role.

Table 1   *Classification of group processes*

Category 1	Basic	Interaction
Category 2	Structural	Group development Social structure Sub-group formation
Category 3	Locomotive	Decision making Purpose and goal formation

Category 4	Molar	Formation of norms, standards,
		    and values
		Development of cohesion
		Development of group pressure
		    (influence)
		Development of climate

Group processes as a function of interaction

If human beings are aware of others then interaction begins. Even ignoring others is a form of interaction in the sense that it is a conscious behaviour motivated by a recognition of the presence of another. Being ignored also generates a response, thus fulfilling the basic two-part nature of interaction as action and re-action. The nature of interaction is so basic that it apparently underlies all the group processes that have been identified.

Where human beings gather together they interact and it is not difficult to see that by interacting, the larger patterns of behaviour, existing after time, which we have called group processes, emerge. Even when we look at the processes as functions of other factors like influence or communication, interaction between persons is the medium of exchange that carries the influence or communication. Often enough the basic nature of the interactive process has led to attempts to say that the whole of the life of a group is a sequence of interactions between individuals taking place in the context of the group and that nothing remotely like a *group* process actually occurs.

Such an argument leads to one of the most interesting continua in the area of group dynamics, the range from contextual use of the group to instrumental use, behind which lies fundamental concepts of human nature. Briefly, at the contextual end is the belief that human influence situations occur as interaction between two people, one as influencer and one as influenced, and that the setting in which this interaction is embedded has only a secondary and peripheral value. At the instrumental end is the belief that the major change agent is a group in its 'formed' state. This implies that change comes from a recognition and an understanding of the need and possibility for change. Changes in perception are much more readily brought about in a group situation than by individual persuasion. There is little possibility of reconciling these poles although the use of techniques that draw from both sources tend to be more efficient in coping with a wider range of need than approaches that are based on one or the other alone.

Attempts to measure interaction are fairly widespread and well known (see Bales 1950, for example). What tends to occur, however, is that some aspect of interaction that is readily available and quantifiable, such as number and nature of vocal interchanges, is used to represent the whole. The possibility of measuring factors such as gesture, posture, or facial expression, all forms of non-verbal communication, is not any greater. The judgement of meaning is liable to much greater error even than the ascription of general meanings to the spoken word.

But it is indisputable that without interaction of some sort it would not be possible to say that a group exists, except in a purely numerical or categorizing sense. Do a number of widely separated individuals who write or phone each other regularly but never meet in person constitute a group? In a vague and uneasy way the answer must be 'no' as the interaction between them cannot easily encompass more than two people at any one time. If each person was available to the others at the same time on video monitors then a more positive interaction would ensue because each member of the group would know that his or her behaviour was immediately visible to the others and they, and everyone else, could see the responses to it directly.

For all practical purposes, group=interaction. Out of interaction grows the awareness of feedback; feedback is the prime stimulus to knowledge of the existence of self, and thus the endeavour to control the elements of the feedback situation to generate the degree of security commensurate with benefit arises, and gives birth to the processes of familiarization, constellation formation, alliances, the development of the rules of this particular game, and the pursuit of given ends.

In producing these effects, others develop. Some factors arise that are special or specific forms of more general processes; others are more diffuse processes arising from some that were originally more precise. Thus, the purposes of the group and its rules of behaviour arise from the more general decision-making processes that are tacitly agreed upon. A sense of belonging, however, which is a rather non-specific feeling, arises out of the practice together over a period of time of more precise forms of behaviour.

Accepting that interaction is fundamental and basic to the group process cannot absolve us from the necessity of noting how group processes may be seen to arise from factors such as influence and communication that lie at a less basic level of human behaviour than interaction. In truth some confusion appears in the literature concerning any distinction between interaction and communication. For instance, Bales's observation categories, called an Interaction Process Analysis, are defined as a procedure to 'classify the pattern and content of communication in a group regardless of its history, function or composition.' (Raven and Rubin 1976 : 508). But interaction is more than the patterns of communication and it is therefore necessary to examine in more detail the claim that it is the generator of processes.

Group processes as a function of group influence

'The key phrase in the preceding paragraph is "social influence". And this becomes our working definition of social psychology: the influences that people have upon the beliefs or behaviour of others.'   (Aronson 1976 : 6)

Psychologists such as Aronson believe that all human interaction constitutes an influence situation. That is, in any relationship between people each is trying to influence the behaviour of some or all of the others by using many different methods and techniques, and each is subject to the influence attempts of others. If this is true then all group processes arise because of attempts to influence the behaviour of others, and interaction is the medium of these attempts.

Once again interaction is the basic factor, but if what every individual attempts to do in any social situation is to maximize his or her satisfaction, then interaction becomes the medium through which satisfactions are obtained. This is not a simple process if only because the needs of individuals, and what, for them, comprises satisfaction of those needs, is not only complex but also not readily available to scrutiny. Later we shall consider the important concept of equilibrium, but it is sufficient to say at this point that satisfaction for individual members in a group situation is dependent upon how much satisfaction they can mediate for others.

Thus, both the individual goals of members and of the group as a unit have to be maintained in some sort of harmonious relationship to each other. The pressure and influence that the group can exert on members therefore have to be balanced by the individual's perception that the costs of submitting to that pressure are less than the rewards to be obtained. If there are alternatives that offer equal satisfaction for less cost, then the member will almost certainly seriously consider changing his or her allegiance. So we have a partially overt bargaining situation in which members trade conformity and service for satisfactions awarded by group membership. All the 'factors-affecting' can then be seen as moves in the complex game of maximization for the simple reason that at many different levels of operation the group can be seen to provide satisfaction for its members.

Let us take one or two examples. A group exists to perform some kind of task. As we have seen, that task, or tasks, must not be one that is better performed by individuals except in very special circumstances. If individuals can perform the task for which the group ostensibly exists, then the prime function of the group is something other than the avowed task. It may be that this prime function is social (pleasure in each others' company, for example), where the avowed task is a kind of payment that the group offers to those who may not remain members if socializing were the sole purpose of the group and yet whose presence socially is a reward for other members.

As members become aware that direct attempts to create satisfactions for themselves in the group are not the sole means of doing so, and may not even be the most important, influence changes towards generating the group as a system that will be more efficient in producing satisfaction for most if not all members. Thus, in the process of development groups demonstrate a movement away from the individuality of members towards acceptance of unity, the discrete elements becoming fused as the realization of the increased benefits available grows. Equally there is a movement away from caution towards other members to open liking and thus to a level of trust.

Sub-group formation is a matter of alliance either to further influence attempts or in order to generate increased security in the company of like-minded members. Constraints are a problem in so far as they facilitate or place limitations on what the group can achieve. In other words, they are factors that influence the exercise of group power. Of course, they can be balanced by group processes that increase satisfactions in other directions.

All other 'factors-affecting' can equally be seen as manifestations of attempts to influence both individual and group. Group processes are the behaviours that are brought into being by attempts to influence the group and its members in the direction of increasing, stabilizing, or continuing satisfactions. The constraints are pre-existing or developing conditions that surround groups and enable or restrict these attempts and thus create boundaries. The sum total of these 'factors-affecting' adds up to the kind, quality, and intensity of the influence that the group can exert, and is the product of them all as interacting, enhancing, or countervailing factors.

Group processes as a function of communication

'A group mediates any communication.'

(Litvak 1967 : 107)

In order to interact with others or influence their behaviour it is necessary to open some form of communication system with them. Litvak's quotation given above indicates that he believes that communication is the central control system of the group. In a very real sense any group defines 'reality' for its members thus *(Figure 1):*

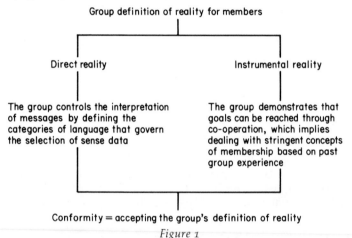

Group definition of reality for members

Direct reality — The group controls the interpretation of messages by defining the categories of language that govern the selection of sense data

Instrumental reality — The group demonstrates that goals can be reached through co-operation, which implies dealing with stringent concepts of membership based on past group experience

Conformity = accepting the group's definition of reality

Figure 1

As conformity offers perhaps the best chance an individual has for maximizing personal goals within the group, this procedure is supported by very powerful motivation. Thus, if a major source of power resides in the group's ability to mediate communication for its members, it is not surprising to discover that the group processes can all be seen to arise as functions of this communication control. In *Group Processes* (Douglas 1979), an analysis of the generative factors of the group processes showed that some form of communication occurred in virtually every one.

Leadership styles can be seen as the ways in which the communication net is controlled. In fact, the more centralized that network is, the more likely it is that a leader will emerge.

Access to the communication network enhances members' attraction to the group; decision making in respect of complex problems is both served by a communication system that is decentralized and accessible where simple problems are better dealt with by a centralized system. The communication system reflects the social structure of a group; free communication facilitates sub-group formations and is directly related to the climate under which the group functions; proximity of members tends to increase communication between them so there is a reciprocal relationship between kinds of communication and the size of the group.

The interdependency between group processes and communication is extensive, in fact overwhelming, and the relationship to group influence is equally powerful. In fact, this latter relationship seems often to have been subsumed under the general rubric of group influence in conformity. However, Deutsch and Gerard (1955) draw a clear distinction between 'normative social influence', which Tajfel (1978) suggests is what most people are referring to when they speak of 'conformity', and 'informational social influence'.[1] The similarity between Deutsch's and Gerard's definition of the latter as the 'influence to accept information obtained from another as evidence about reality' and the starting point of this discussion would seem to indicate that communication effects on group processes are essentially a definable part of the group influence situation.

A more profitable approach is in the argument that the dyadic relationship is fundamentally the basis of all group formation. Smith (1978) argues that the pair is the basic form of communication and that when two people are interacting they necessarily exclude others apart from being aware of their presence. In this way, groups are seen as a kaleidoscope of dyadic communications

[1] Allen (1965) saw the maximum effect of normative social influence and informational social influence occurring when members of a group were in an interdependent state, i.e. when they are dependent upon one another to achieve common or group goals. This has particular relevance for the degree of group pressure that a team can exert because of the co-operation required to achieve successful outcomes and also because of the interpretation of reality that the team creates for its members.

with a more or less imposed order derived from the way they change and in the emphasis given to their being maintained and repeated.

Indeed, it is possible to argue that all group processes are the outcome of dyadic communications. For instance, the development of a group can be seen to be related directly to the number, frequency, and results of dyadic relationships that have occurred. If all group members have communicated reciprocally with each other, then, if those communications have been rewarding, an increased knowledge and familiarity will have arisen and the shared nature of the group's experience will have increased.

Smith says, 'it is axiomatic and empirically demonstrable that the individual is capable of engaging no more than one person in genuine dialogue – total reciprocity – in an existential moment. This universally inherited human limitation renders the dyadic interactional network indispensible to group process' (Smith 1978 : 302).

THE TOTAL 'FACTORS-AFFECTING' (PROCESSES, CONSTRAINTS, LEADERSHIP ACTS)

'The group we study is not only *interactive* it is also *dynamic*. It is a group whose members are continuously *changing* and *adjusting* relationships with reference to one another.'

(Bonner 1959 : 4)

The immediate facts that face an observer of any group are the direct behavioural interactions of its members. However, it soon becomes clear that a large number of factors that are not at first sight obvious are affecting the here-and-now behaviour, the current patterns of interaction. The presence of an individual member in any group constitutes a series of more or less short periods of time in the ongoing line of his or her life. He or she reacts to the perceptions of these transient milieux and the people they contain with behavioural insights gained from other such transient occupations of a group-member role. In time the current experience will be data added to the repertoire of experience and may or may not have become the occasion for a modification of perceptions and responses in group situations.

Group processes have been described as the larger patterns of behaviour that a group of such pre-programmed individuals will produce. The group has some possibility of generating new experience and thus of presenting members with opportunities for change; it has also the possibility of confirming members in their existing behaviour. But in any case, group processes as defined here relate to the group as a functioning unit and not to the individual behaviour patterns of which the processes are composed.

Reference has also been made to leadership acts and constraints as important elements of the dynamics of a group. Leadership acts are only a special variety of ordinary membership behaviour. The special nature derives from two particular attributes. First, there is a larger than ordinary awareness of the nature of leadership acts on the part of the performer and of their possible consequences. Second, there is a conscious use of intervention skills based on a desire to influence the group in known ways.

There is nothing fundamentally different in this kind of behaviour from that of the most ignorant (of group dynamics, that is) member of a group. It is a question of degree, of knowledge, and skill. From our experiences, we are all endowed with the knowledge of the consequences of our behavioural inputs, but that knowledge is most usually personal, restricted, and limited to our own stored memories. Also, it tends to be unsystematic. The growth of effective leadership for all members of a group stems from a widening knowledge of causal relationships, an increase in the certainty of being able to influence desired outcomes, and a more structured knowledge system. However leadership acts are performed within a group, they constitute one of the major determinants of the nature of that group and of its life and performance.

Virtually anything that exists has the potential to influence human behaviour and by no means always at the level of consciousness. There is no way in which all the possible influence systems and objects can be given adequate consideration, not only because of the large number involved, but also because the possible effects change as the group changes. For example, an atmosphere set up by a cold and unwelcoming building may have an overwhelming effect in the beginning stages of a group when member commitment is low. It may be totally ignored later when members have become immersed in the group activity. The constraint is the same but the perception of it, and thus its effect, are different.

However, to ignore major constraining factors as sources of influence on a group is by no means equal to disposing of them. On the contrary, whatever effect they are likely to produce will still occur at some level of intensity but it will tend to be masked by being regarded as the outcome of some factor to which the group is paying attention.

Thus, group processes, leadership acts, and the constraints are seen as 'factors-affecting' the establishment, development, and outcome of group behaviour. This introduces a kind of double bind in several ways. In a sense, group processes, that is, the constituents of group processes, pre-exist any given group in the programming that any individual has received. But any group is a unique situation and the processes it develops are a growth out of, and different from, the programming that created them. Group processes are chickens *and* eggs. The same kind of before-and-after nature exists for leadership acts. Constraints have a more than double nature in that they may or may not be immutable. Also, their effect can be positive-supportive or nega-tive-restrictive. In any case, apart from the actual material nature of some constraints, the way they are perceived at any given moment in the life of a group may have substantially disparate consequences.

Nevertheless, the assumption made here is that groups that arise as a matter of everyday life, the so-called 'natural' groups, must be affected by these factors in the ways outlined above. Given that human beings continue to congregate in groups in order to achieve certain reasonably well-defined ends, the nature of the groups that arise should provide ample evidence of how the 'factors-affecting' have been dealt with, and, in turn, should provide methods or rules by which groups that are deliberately created to achieve limited purposes can be designed to maximize the chances of successful outcomes. Some of the so-called 'natural' groups are, of course, 'created'. But the point is that they were not created as 'groups' in the sense of a knowledge of what the dynamics of groups could achieve, but as traditional instruments having a historical precedent of a given success rate.

PART TWO

The Probable Effects of Group Processes in 'Natural' Groups

INTRODUCTION

'The solutions to common problems become embodied in the culture and in the norms of groups, and are enforced as the approved way of doing things, such as how to make canoes or aircraft. There is a kind of social evolution whereby the best solutions survive.'   (Argyle 1972 : 107)

Given that the description of group processes consists of isolating and naming those parts of an overall group process that can be readily identified, it must follow that all the group processes are present in any human assemblage. In different kinds of human groupings it also follows that the relative stress placed upon each of the processes or the relative importance in which they are held should be the factor that decides the particular nature of the group.

Often enough the process that is taken to be the one that determines the nature of any particular group is that which determines the purpose for which the group exists. However, such is the nature of group processes that the means by which that purpose is effected may be much more a determinant of the character of the group than the purpose it is aiming to achieve.

Take a group that is set up to make decisions. Its purpose is to arrive at decisions; it is a decision-making group. Its purpose is clear. But the manner in which it makes its decisions may be a much more characteristic feature than the purpose. In fact, an observer may often be unaware of the central purpose of any particular group, but be impressed by the nature of the social structure it has, that is, the status, roles, and positions occupied by the members.

In order to examine this thesis it is only necessary to look at groups that have been characterized as 'natural' and to see whether it is possible to isolate not just the group processes in action but also the relative degree of importance these different processes have in contributing to the performance of these 'natural' groups. If it can be shown, even in a reasonably crude form, that group processes are emphasized or de-emphasized in different ways in different 'natural' groups seeking the most efficient performance, then we must have the possibility of formulating a guide to the intensity, sequence, and duration of those processes that tend to produce given group outcomes.

Now it must be obvious from the foregoing that any analysis based solely on the group processes that are the internal dynamics of a group can never produce a wholly satisfactory set of answers to the questions of why a 'natural' group operates in one way rather than another to achieve its desired outcome. It is essential to include also the factors that affect the internal dynamics of the group in order to upgrade the quality of the answer one can eventually devise. Although this necessarily complicates the issues involved, the constraints must be considered. Let us take an example.

It has been stressed already that the relative duration of a group process as an important factor may vary considerably from group to group and function at different stages in the life of any one group. Straight away, the constraint of time becomes a salient distinguishing feature. The length of time, or the frequency that eventually turns out to be most suited to the achievement of the group's task, tends to be arrived at by trial and error (the 'kind of social evolution' mentioned by Argyle in the quotation at the head of this introduction).

Part Two sets out to discover what the process of 'social evolution' has arrived at in terms of natural groups whose functions are relatively easy to understand. Then in Part Four I want to show what advantage 'created' groups can reap from understanding the relationship between processes and performance provided by the evolution of 'natural' groups.

One final point concerns performance. Because groups have arisen as it were spontaneously to meet given situations, then logically one should expect to find clear indications that groups perform certain functions better than individuals. Also, when these functions are identified they will bear a significant correlation to the functions that 'natural' groups have been developed to perform.

Below is a brief list (drawn from the review sources indicated) of the factors that are seen to be more effectively performed by a group than by separate individuals. The list is task oriented and, for the sake of clarity, ignores all the maintenance functions of a group in assessing whether the correlation with 'natural' groups noted above actually exists. For example, any successful 'natural' group (and perhaps the only criterion we have of success is that the form of the group continues to be used over long periods of time to deal with particular situations) should show a high presentation of those functions listed in *Table 2*.[2] It is also

Table 2 *Functions that groups perform better than individuals*

1	Tasks requiring more than one person.
2	Tasks requiring the division of labour.
3	By combining estimates, groups reduce possible error.
4	Groups produce more and better solutions to a problem.
5	Groups make a more efficient use of resources.
6	Groups eliminate inferior ideas more effectively.
7	Social motivation is higher in the presence of others.
8	The presence of others leads to increased productivity.
9	Where tasks involving random error are in process, groups tend to produce superior judgements.
10	Groups achieve more than even the most superior individual member.
11	Groups learn faster.
12	Groups tend to make more risky decisions.
13	Groups minimize the sense of responsibility of any one member for the outcome.
14	Groups ensure tenacity of purpose by committing members to group decisions.
15	The feedback of performance is from multiple sources and is therefore likely to be more accurate.
16	Involvement and participation produces a high level of commitment.

[2] The sources of information for *Table 2* are as follows: Collins and Guetzkow (1964); Davis (1969); Hare (1962); Levanway (1972); McGrath and Altman (1966); Shaw (1971); and Tafjel and Fraser (1978).

possible that some situations may be dealt with more efficiently by a combination of individual and group contribution, bearing in mind what areas each performs more efficiently. Some of the factors shown in *Table 2* are indisputable, some, like the ability of groups to take riskier decisions than individuals, are challenge-able;[3] some are common sense (for example, tasks requiring more than one person are by definition a group exercise); still others are so constrained in area as to have only small interest. The overall ideas, however, are reasonably substantiated.

Table 2 can usefully be compared with *Table 3*, derived from Smith (1980:13). Smith was listing the attributes of working with groups and working with individuals that would, he felt, allow a choice between methods for use in any particular in-stance. *Table 3* shows clearly the potential differences of the two methods and serves to reinforce the ideas discussed earlier in this introduction. For further comparison it is instructive to give a brief list of tasks that individuals have been shown to perform better than groups (*Table 4*).

Table 3   *Some attributes of group work compared to work with individuals*

	Group work	Individual work
Utilization of leader resources	Economical	Intensive
Potential responsiveness to the needs of individual client	Moderate	High
Clients choice of models from whom to learn	High	Low
Problems in scheduling sessions finding appropriate setting	High	Low
Potential for continuing support from other clients	High	Low
Minimum time required for effective work	High	Low

[3] It has, in fact, been challenged. See the discussion in Raven and Rubin (1976) and Walker (1974). Walker says, 'at the very least this should caution against an unconditional acceptance of the notion that groups hold a distinct advantage over single individuals in decision-making tasks' (1974:127).

Table 4 *Conditions for superior performance by individuals*

1	Where it is difficult to demonstrate the solution to others.
2	Where an individual would be unhindered by the status hierarchy or conformity pressures of a group.
3	Where speed of response is crucial – an individual is often faster – he or she does not have to consider other opinions.
4	Where time is crucial (e.g. economies).
5	Where the presence of others would be inhibiting.
6	Where an individual skill is crucial.
7	Where creativity is important (e.g. artistic design).

In Chapter 2 the concept of the 'natural' group was discussed and the idea was aired that groups so designated had a large element of spontaneity involved in their origins and in this sense were different from groups that were consciously designed or created to meet some specific need.

This section of the book will look at groups that have a greater or lesser content of 'naturalness', as defined above, in their make-up. Thus, we start with the family, where the elements of design, that is, of conscious design, may be said to be negligible. There are arguments against regarding the family as an entirely natural feature, at least in the form it currently assumes. However, discussion of how much the family is a product of the society that encompasses it is almost irrelevant in respect of the biological family group, this particular function being the main factor in family organization in any case. No one can totally ignore the societal factors involved in shaping the family but in the scale of the naturalness of groups, the family must be given pride of place.

Second, I look at groups composed of friends. Such groups appear in all societies and at all periods of history, and the relationship of friends has a very long and natural history. Once again, the nature of such groups is obviously exposed to influence from the kind of society in which it occurs, but the element of 'naturalness' is dominant.

The other three groups that I examine in this section have a much greater element of conscious design about them, but they have in common the fact that only recently have they been subject to scrutiny in terms of the dynamics of the groups that they so obviously are. Work groups, teams, and committees have often only been regarded as men and women associating to perform a task. They also have in common a transient nature, that is, their existence is directly related to the time-span necessary to perform a given function, which often requires quite a short time. But they also have a long historical tradition that the newer concept of specifically 'created' groups does not have and this is a crucial point.

Work groups, teams, and committees are groups that have traditionally arisen to meet certain kinds of situation; families and friendship groups could also be defined in this way but with a much larger element of 'naturalness' in their make-up. The fact that a long history of reported use of these forms of groups exists would tend to indicate that they fulfil the purposes for which they arise with a reasonable degree of efficiency.

For that reason alone, we should want to ask why such groups work. For example, what combination of dynamics creates a good team? Even more rewarding would be to discern the elements of design and combination that underlie their continued successful use. These elements would then show what the processes of group design are and how they might best be used.

Part Three will pick up this thread in looking at how well design elements have been used in selected 'created' groups, thus rounding off the investigation of design factors begun here. The basic elements of the investigation are these group processes and 'factors-affecting' described in Chapters 2 and 3, and it is the patterns of combination and use of these factors that will be seen to be the design elements we seek to isolate.

4

THE FAMILY

INTRODUCTION

'What is probably the most important kind of small group in human society is often overlooked by small group researchers – and consequently there are important features of the family group which have never been embodied in small group experiments or theorising.'   (Argyle 1969 : 240)

It is not the purpose here either to trace the historical development of the family or to argue its merits and demerits as a social unit, but merely to show that given certain functions the family operates as a group. Its group nature is very different from most other social groups and herein lies advantage and disadvantage.

The latter arises because in some areas of the family the functions are so different in comparison with other groups that its general 'group' nature can be challenged. Take the simple example of how people tend to become members of a group. They join voluntarily, or they find themselves a member by circumstance, or sometimes they are compelled to become a member. Most of these membership forms are of calculable duration – often short – and there is no pre-existing special relationship to other members. The family, on the other hand, is in existence before its current members. Everyone is a member of a family of origin, becomes a member of another family by voluntary act of will, and, as the result of the passing of time, is then subjected to changes of role within both family groups.

Families are unique as groups for many reasons, but two stand out as having the most difference from other group forms: the relationship of blood ties, and the perpetual nature of the family. To these one could add the universality of some form of family organization and the very powerful role the family plays in shaping the kind of human beings that emerge through the process of socialization.

In tracing the historical growth of the concept of childhood, Ariès (1973) also shows how the family has had a changing role in society. Notably he points to the increase in the private nature of family life but more noticeably in current society to the transfer of many functions to external bodies, and a diminution in the size of the family unit. One example must suffice of this change, the education of children. This demonstrates clearly that an external system (e.g. school) has taken over a considerable area of what once must have been the responsibility of the family. Indeed, the school now often enough offers attitudes and experiences that are not necessarily those of the parent figures, and can, and does, engender conflict between the two principal sub-groups that form any family.

In Western society the state also assumes some responsibility for the standard of care in families, provides sanctions against those who fall below minimal standards, and offers alternative forms of care where necessary. This diminution of the overall power and authority of the senior sub-group in a family has gone alongside the reduction of the size of the family unit which has effectively concentrated the remaining power in the family in fewer hands and reduced the number of those experienced enough to be consulted or asked for help within its ambit. What would once have to have been considered as an integral part of the family group can now quite satisfactorily be regarded as a network in which the family group is embedded. This tends to highlight the nuclear family group and emphasizes the nature of the two principal sub-groups, parents and children, of which it is formed. This division is not absolute, nor does it effectively prevent large areas of family behaviour occurring as unit activity.

The advantages arising from the nature of the family group are found in exactly the areas that also produce disadvantage, that is, the intensity of contact and the duration of the group. Because of these factors, the dynamics of the family as a group appear to be writ large and often crisis highlights certain aspects very clearly. Without question, our experience of family life has generated the criteria, the processes by which we describe and study the dynamics of other groups. There are countless references in group literature to processes in 'created' groups that are like those in the family. It would be surprising if there were not. Given different levels of intensity of attraction, take away the kinship and blood ties, and the family stands as the prototype for all our current group experience.

Whatever family dynamics can be isolated, however much they may then be useful in the creation and understanding of other groups (often designed to undo and/or re-do some of the effects families have on their members), and however basic such dynamics turn out to be, we cannot ignore the ways in which the role of the family has changed. Nor can we ignore ideas that it does not function effectively to generate the best use of human potential. We have also to consider, as in Mary Kenny's article quoted below, that there may be some very seriously bad results emanating from the family as the source of socialization.

'More than a quarter of British marriages now end in divorce. There are close on a million one-parent families. The number of teenagers in trouble with the law has more than doubled over the past decade. Illegitimacy rates in England and Scotland are now at their highest rates ever. There is an unprecedented number of children in care.' (Kenny 1981)

The amount of literature about the family is enormous, encompassing the concern there has always been about what has been described as the basic structural unit of human society. For instance, Ariès (1973) in *Centuries of Childhood* thought that the family was indeed a very successful and powerful institution. He believed that the current concept of 'the family' was remarkably modern and also that what it produced was an 'intolerance towards variety, the same insistence on uniformity'. He wrote of the family as so powerful an institution that it could stifle both open and public relations. Our concern is with the way the family functions as a group and how effective its use of group processes may be in the movement towards its stated goals and in the exercise of its power.

THE DISTINCTIVE NATURE OF THE FAMILY AS A GROUP

'The family we are born into is the small group to which most of us owe our primary allegiance for the first fifteen or twenty years of our life, and, indeed for many people in our society, it remains a focus for allegiance throughout their lives.'

(Tajfel 1978 : 179)

Murray Bowen (1966) wrote, 'The family is a system in that change in one part of the system is followed by compensatory change in other parts'. He was talking about the factor of equilibrium that is a function of relatively stable groups and is often used as a fundamental defining feature of a group.

Throughout small group literature the close comparison of 'created' groups with the family abounds. Beukenkamp (1952) notes that as psychotherapy groups enter stage three in their development (the stage of cohesion), the members tend to relive their family experience or begin to realize that they are becoming members of a 'new' family – the therapy group. Whiteley and Gordon (1979) quote Yalom as saying that the group in therapy resembles the family. Maybe what they are saying is that what happens in the family is the paradigm for all future group experiences; that we find it difficult, if not impossible, to use group concepts that are not based on those revealed in the family.

One way to highlight distinction is by comparison. There have been, and are, other ways of bringing up children than the family group, either nuclear or extended. One such way, which has been well recorded, is the system of child care in the Israeli Kibbutz. Bettelheim (1969) analysed the main factors of the Kibbutz organization and presented a critique of the end results. Because the concept of equal worth was paramount, a situation designed to help women to overcome the role of childbearer and carer was created. Children were removed from the mother four days after the birth and cared for communally, thereby effectively removing them from being part of a family, of being subjected to over-possessive behaviour, and used as bargaining counters in marital squabbles. They became, in essence, members of a group without the major factors that create the special nature of the family group.

The advantages of such a system may be listed as follows:

1 Every child is given the same chance in life as every other. The differences of genetic endowment are recognized.
2 No one opts out. The community is totally responsible.
3 There are no differences in material possessions.
4 There is no evidence of cruelty and violence.
5 There are few serious mental disturbances, or sex crimes. There is no open homosexuality, and no drug problem.
6 There is little evidence of jealousy or bitter rivalry. There is no neglect.
7 Each member has a secure place in the community for the whole of his or her life.

This is a very different list from one that could be compiled about the family group, and the disadvantages of Kibbutz life are perhaps even more revealing:

1 The system produces conformists. There is little disagreement, and equally little ability to see other points of view.
2 There is an inability to hold an opinion different from that held by the majority.
3 There is no room for rebellion.
4 Emotional flatness develops. Children are unable to make deep, loving relationships.
5 Children are deprived of intimate contact with any adult with whom they wish to identify.
6 Repression and suppression operate in order to produce conformity. This generates inward tensions, which are unexpressed.

7   The growth of outstanding people is restricted due to lack of
    flexibility.

The pressures to conform are huge. Satisfaction levels may
well be high but, as a result, many of the factors that stem from
the unequal life of family groups, such as difference, ambition,
and emotional range, are stifled, or rather not developed, in
favour of attributes that make for equality and the smooth
functioning of the community.

By eradicating some of the most important features, the
Kibbutz movement demonstrated quite clearly the distinctive
features that a family produces. The differences are striking.
What a society needs in its members produces the kind of
child-bearing practices that produce the society. The problem has
always been that the arrangements of family life have seemed
immutable and natural. The Kibbutz movement showed on a
large scale that this was not really true and in the process
highlighted more precisely what the family group actually produced.

THE PRINCIPAL DYNAMICS OF THE FAMILY GROUP AS
GROUP PROCESSES AND THEIR PROBABLE EFFECTS

'The whole evolution of our contemporary manners is unin-
telligible if one neglects this astonishing growth of the concept
of the family. It is not individualism which has triumphed, but
the family.'   (Ariès 1973 : 393)

Interaction

The interrelationships in the family are complex, subtle, changing over time, and present many of the features of a formal
organization. The major factors involved have already been
mentioned – the long history of relationships and interaction
that every family has, and the special nature of the bonds that lie
at the base of these interactions.

The time factor ensures that the nature of the interaction
within a family will change. Thus, the totally dominant rela-

tionship of parents to small children has to change to an interaction of equals as the children move towards adulthood and eventually leave, usually to found their own family. Until the point of departure (either physical or psychological), the family is a closed unit with a single base functioning at a high level of intimacy and in close physical proximity one with another. Many activities are shared; some remain the prerogative of individual members but are still pursued within the network of the family and obviously have an effect upon other members. Interaction is closely connected with joint activities: living together, sleeping, eating, and playing in each other's company, often within the confines of an environment that is recognized as 'home'. Affection, feelings of obligation, care, and concern for the good of other members often operate at a high level and so conflict, when it comes, is often violent. Aggression, affection, and emotional violence are more intense than in other groups.

The familial bond is unique; the sense of belonging is of great importance and may well be the basis for all subsequent feelings of being a member of other groups. Even when family bonds are greatly weakened by time, separation, or rejection, the formative effect of early family interaction is still there, and the family may also become the first and perhaps the most important reference group. In essence, the family is the yardstick by which all future and current group experiences tend to be judged.

Development

The changes in the family group can be enormous first because it exists for such a long period of time and, second, because its membership changes both in terms of age and of presence in the family home. The major development is one brought about by the change in the nature of the relationship of one major sub-group, the parents, to the other major sub-group, the children. As children can arrive in the family throughout a fairly large part of its existence, the development of the family is often complicated by the need to retrace and re-enact relationships that, for other members of the group, are well in the past. Thus, the dynamic of development is constantly shifting its base as new

members are added. Where members stabilize early in the
family's history then development follows the course of the
maturation process. Indeed, the development of created groups is
often described in terms of this process, growing into each other
and adapting to change while maintaining the basic affiliative and
affectionate needs intact.

Structure

As has already been said, the family has a formal organization
that often enough owes a great deal to tradition, culture, and the
kind of society in which the family is located. The structure is one
of the exercise of power, of positions and roles, and the ways of
behaving that are attached to them, the latter being socially
recognized. Of course, the kinship structure is an important part,
which is mainly a stable one, but the roles within the family, like
most of the other processes, change over time.

Argyle (1969) suggests that the family can be seen as a system
containing four or six principal roles. If the latter, then sometimes some of the role positions may not be filled. It is true that
while the name attached to these role positions is invariable, the
structure of power, authority, affection, and influence they
represent may vary markedly over the period of existence of the
members concerned.

Sub-group formation

The two major sub-groupings within the family have already
been indicated. Clearly the relationship of parent/child and
child/child are of significantly different orders and are fundamental to the biological nature of human beings. Alliances
within the family may be formed across this fundamental division and occasionally, despite deep taboos, incestuous relationships occur. Often enough other temporary or even more
permanent groupings occur on the basis of sex, age, or affection,
which also cut across the major sub-grouping. Where the family
group is larger than the basic nuclear family then many more
permanent sub-groups are possible – grandparents, uncles,
aunts, and other kinship structures. In societies other than those

of Western culture, and at other times, many of these sub-groups have formed much more important parts of the essential family structure giving a much wider base to the number of relationships a child could have still within the compass of his or her family.

Group goals

The goals of the family group are essentially to maintain the group; provide for the security, well-being, and physical and emotional needs of the members; and to produce, rear, and socialize children. Lesser goals may involve the effective organization of the group in the performance of tasks, domestic jobs, and the numerous aspects of maintaining discipline and good relations within the family.

Decision making

Decision making within the family is a process reflected in the dominance/submission patterns that are held reasonably static by the influence of culture and tradition. These can change through economic circumstances, the influence of particularly powerful or weak personalities, and changes in the status of members *vis-à-vis* other members. Decision making, while structurally determined within fairly broad bounds by the factors mentioned, is often best described in terms of spheres of influence with a discernible trend in Western Europe towards a more democratic basis for decisions of major importance, though legal responsibility for some decisions is vested in some members of the family and not others.

Norms, standards, and values

These are very much dictated by the standards of the larger society in which the family is embedded. The range is wide in tolerant societies and very restricted and critically patterned in others. The family is a primary reference group for how things are done and the style of life. It has a shared outlook, its own rituals for meals, holidays, and anniversaries, and ideas about how leisure is spent. Within the family there is little self-presentation; there is a clearly articulated role structure; status is based upon age and to some extent sex; and there is a whole accumulation of norms derived from tradition and the immediate and wider culture.

Cohesion

Cohesion is dependent upon a unique bonding built through kinship ties and entails many claims and obligations, and a structure of power relations, all of which are strongly affectional in nature and different in their quality and intensity from the cohesive bonds of other groups.

Influence

In the family group, influence is exercised in many different ways. As far as the younger members are concerned the family influence establishes a pattern of future behaviour; parental standards are absorbed and remain a focus of allegiance that can affect the development of sexual, affective, and parental behaviour. The whole range of influence factors from moral persuasion, through role-modelling to primary intervention are in use. The effect of warmth and rejection, of identification, of structure, permissiveness and discipline, whether consistent or not, are also major influence factors.

Climate

Climate is an immensely variable factor ranging from effective meshing together to cold ritual, non-interactive coexistence. But the main features are privacy and intimacy.

Environment

This is so vast an area of possible effects that its main features can only be hinted at. Thus, the society in which the family exists, with all its patterns, habits and traditions, their religion, geographical and occupational mobility, class, and economic state, are all powerful affecting factors. So too are the physical environment, crowding, living conditions, climate, availability of the necessities of life, and the aggression or otherwise of neighbours.

Membership

Membership of a family is like no other membership of a group in that it comprises blood relationships and pair bondings between man and woman. The essential nature of the blood relationship is that it is in continuous existence from the moment of creation, although later it may be rejected and unacknowledged. The younger members of a family have both a dependent relationship to parents and sibling relationships that are often essentially competitive. The parent members have sexual and companionate relationships with each other and protective and nurturant relationships to children and often to other dependents. The principle of group membership for the individuals who comprise a family is often strong enough never to be thought about and is then taken for granted.

Time

Time, as a constraint, is everlasting. Membership of a family is for ever; the bonds are long lasting whether or not a member later becomes estranged or becomes a member of another family.

Resources

The resources of a family vary so much over such an enormous range that they may hardly be defined. Likewise, its *size* can comprise a minimum of three to maxima of hundreds stretching across generations and laterally through intermarriage. In most senses families are *closed* groups. Access is by birth, marriage, fostering, and adoption. Its *activity* is mainly that of a mutual support system with survival and child-rearing as its main functions.

Leadership

Leadership behaviour is related to different members of the family at different times and may be traditionally, culturally, socially, religiously, or personally determined. There are, of course, class variations in responsibility and authority structures but in general leadership includes task and maintenance functions and tends to be co-operatively functional.

Selection

In a family, selection can only relate to the choice of original marriage partners and to the adoption of other members into the family unit. All other family members are born into it and the relationship is of blood ties.

The unique nature of the family as a group should now be clear. As our first and strongest experience of group interaction, the family forms the basis of our response to all subsequent groups until new learning creates the possibility of different response patterns. However, because the relationship within the family group is so different from later group experience, it is necessary at this stage to examine briefly the idea that dyadic relationships are the fundamental basis of group interaction and then to look at the concept of equilibrium.

DYADIC INTERACTION

'It is here postulated that the two-person interactional system is the necessary condition for connecting the individual and the group and for effecting a truly functional group process. This suggests in essence that the group is a function of the dyadic relation which in turn is a function of the monadic unit or individual.'   (Smith 1978 : 293)

Satir (1967), in her book *Conjoint Family Therapy*, insisted that a relationship or interpersonal communication between three or more people was a myth and that the basic relationship was dyadic, any third person operating as observer. The components of the dyad are constantly shifting. For example, in the group ABC, the dyad/isolate arrangement may be A, BC; AB, C; or A+B+C. Such an argument depends upon the basic assumption of what constitutes a relationship or a communication. Smith (1978) maintains that only when a genuine dialogue takes place are both parties mutually included. A third party, or others, can be an observer to this reciprocal exchange but, except in a very general sense, they are not included. Other kinds of communication lose the element of direct reciprocity and become what Smith calls 'monologues' or 'technical dialogues'.

As with the concept of balance, which we will discuss next, the basic nature of dyadic relationships shows clearly in the dynamics of the family group because of the special bonding that exists there. The original founders of a family group are a pair. The introduction of one child doubles the pair relationships possible and the addition of other members increases the pair relationships possible by the number of other members of the family. For tasks, for security, for affection, for the expression of anger, and for all the things that the family do, alliances of pairs form, change, and re-form according to circumstances and perceptions.

It is interesting that all these changing pairings, some of which are much more stable and durable than others, are clearly recognized in Freudian psychology. More interesting still is that there is an even clearer sense in which all the dyadic relationships are held within the orbit of the larger unit, the family group. This limiting concept allows the freedom to generate dyadic relationships because all the people within the group have very strong ties of blood, affection, and loyalty to the same unit. The structure is loose enough to allow such dyadic formations but strong enough to contain them in some high degree of security. When members physically leave the family group the loss is not only of the individual, but also in the number of possible relationships that could be formed. The family is relationally impoverished.

All groups show the dyadic relationships but not all have the special relationship of members that allows freedom for the dyads to form and re-form to meet different contingencies. Family dynamics demonstrate what level of relationship is necessary for such flexible response to take place. Even where family relationships are severely restricted by a traditional cultural code, the very constraints serve to illustrate the importance of the overall relationship by the drastic loss of freedom to move within the unit and the equally drastic reduction of flexibility of response that causes the family members to be sacrificed on the altar of tradition or cultural practice.

Now we must discuss the concept of equilibrium or balance in groups and in particular in the family group.

The concept of balance or equilibrium is important in all groups; but it can be most clearly demonstrated in the family. Moreover, in line with what has been said previously, the experience of how or how much equilibrium is maintained in the original family group may be the factor that establishes the individual's degree of need for harmony in all future groups.

Balance is not the static concept it first appears to be. It is not the immovable agreement between different forces in a situation except at a given moment in time. It is better understood as a state of almost continuous adjustment that creates balance within given limits of tolerance. Of course, these limits change as new factors enter. A group is a dynamic entity; new higher or lower, or just different, levels of balance are re-established that integrate as far as possible the new elements. *Figure 2* shows this process diagrammatically. It shows clearly how adjustment to changed circumstances takes place, how the diversion of energy from performance to re-establishing balance occurs, and how balance is eventually restored. Balance in this context is 'Stasis', that is, the point where the individual satisfactions of the group members are at the maximum achievable level given the circumstances. This means that to increase the satisfactions of any one member would automatically bring a corresponding decrease in satisfaction for one or more other members.

Families are subject to many changes in that members grow and change, physically depart or return, and yet always have a psychological presence even when absent. Without doubt, each such occurrence disturbs the level of balance. Often enough readjustment is difficult to make, especially if the previous balance was either high in satisfaction or of long-term duration, or both. The sense of loss at the departure of a member is not entirely due to personal grief but is always accompanied by a realization, if only a felt one, that an ongoing system has been

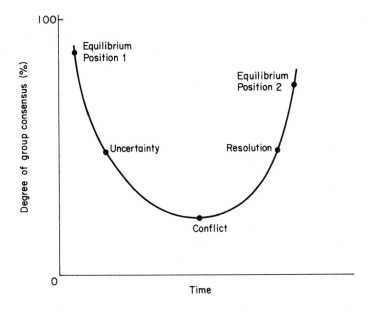

Figure 2 The restoration of group equilibrium

The stable points of equilibrium exist long enough to be recognized as constituting a position within the developmental sequence or dynamic existence of the group. Thus, if EQ 1 is higher than EQ 2, the group is losing cohesion and its ability to work as a unit is being eroded; more time and energy having to be spent in maintenance tactics. If EQ 1 had been lower then EQ 2, an increase in cohesion would have been apparent and more energy available for devoting to the group task.

Source: Chapple and Coon (1965).

destroyed and will need considerable effort to reshape to a new functional normality. Because the bonds of the family group are unique in group dynamics, this element of restructuring after loss is much more readily noticeable. In fact, if the loss is great the group may never re-form because either too great a resource has been lost and cannot be replaced and/or too great an effort would be required to restructure the group.

A problem facing many who work with families is the exact assessment of the satisfactions that generate the current state of equilibrium. Sometimes any balance is hard to see – it often looks like an extremely obvious case of imbalance. Then when efforts are made to redress this imbalance in favour of the apparently suffering parties, or party, the balance that was there all the time is revealed in the disintegration that follows. Of course some balances are achieved at very high cost to some members and equally high rewards for others. But it is still an incredibly difficult piece of social and psychological accounting to establish why such a situation is, and has been, maintained. If the 'put upon' members (a pejorative observer assumption maybe?) cannot see alternatives that may be available to them, then the balance is being maintained by that ignorance. If, however, such members know of the alternatives and choose not to take them, then the balance is being maintained by satisfactions that we can infer but not know about.

The dynamic of equilibrium, the steady state, shows very clearly in the family group where bonds are close and strong. From it we can draw conclusions about the nature of equilibrium in all groups and of the level of satisfaction that is necessary to cope with pressure to conform.

SUMMARY

This chapter has looked at the family as a group. Given that the family is a particular kind of group with a unique position and power in our society, it should follow that an analysis of the dynamics of the family would reveal a selective use of certain processes.

In the general analysis of 'factors-affecting' that followed, it emerges that this assumption is correct. Interaction, sub-group formation, norms, standards, values, and group pressures are revealed as highly important issues. Indeed, the changes of power over time show clearly enough that only a group that supplies a very high level of reward satisfaction has the capacity to exert a great deal of pressure for conformity on its members.

In the early stages of the growth of child members, this power is the central feature in the socializing process.

The chapter ends with a brief statement on dyadic relationships and on the concept of equilibrium. The former is postulated as the essential intermediate step from individual to group, so remarkably revealed in the process of establishing a 'new' family. The latter is discussed as a factor present in all stable groups but not often as clearly visible as it is in a family group.

5

FRIENDSHIP GROUPS

INTRODUCTION

'Idem velle atque idem nolle, ea demum firma amicitia est.'

(Sallust)

Sallust (86–34 BC) went straight to the point of friendship when he wrote in *Catiline* that 'Friendship is to desire and to dislike the same thing'.

Writing about adolescent friendship groups, Argyle (1969) noted that the members of such a group were 'brought together primarily through interpersonal motivations and attractions, not through concern with any task'. Lundberg and Lawsing (1937) described friendship groups as 'voluntary social groupings' and as 'social nuclei'. They believed that social nucleation of this kind had a very great influence on the community in which it existed.

Perhaps the harder we look for the reason for the formation of friendship groups, the more clearly we shall see both their informal nature and the kind of needs they satisfy. Paramount among these will perhaps be the need to share not just activities but also ideas, and to seek for affirmation of identity. Into this matrix must be introduced the ideas of liking and affiliation.

The reasons why people like one another are not too difficult to define. Nicholson (1977) listed six factors in the formation of friendships:

1 The need for stimulation or arousal.
2 Reassurance: the need for confirmation of values, attitudes, and to gain support for the image we have of ourselves.

3 Similarity: we tend to like people who are like us.
4 Recognition that friendship relationships are expendable.
5 Proximity: we tend to like people whom we meet regularly (in essence this also contains the idea of availability) and we cannot really like people we never have any opportunity to meet.
6 Physical attractiveness: usually stronger earlier in our lives before we begin to use non-physical assets as the basis of our assessments of others.

That these factors of attraction are important is indisputable but the process of attraction is not as simple as they would imply. Take for instance the added complication of time. Nicholson and others point out that dissimilarity of attitudes seems to occur frequently in friendships that have existed for only a short time. Quite the reverse is true of long-standing friendships where similar views are the rule.

Gahagan (1975) suggests that it could be argued that friendship groups are at the margins of the definition of a group in that they have an extrinsic goal, output, or shared activities (see *Figure 3*), but they can, and do, bring about changes in individual members. Friendship groups, she adds, 'do not usually study or consciously focus on their relationships with, and experiences of one another'. Such study is an integral part of personal relationship groups.

Argyle (1969) says that adolescent friendship groups 'are probably the only natural groups that discuss social interaction'. Argyle's point is that if social interaction is almost the sole reason for the existence of a friendship group, then the satisfaction members get from being members can be enhanced by keeping the interpersonal relationship behaviour under constant scrutiny first to prevent damaging relationships developing and, second, to promote good (that is, satisfying) ones by recognition and encouragement.

THE NATURE OF FRIENDSHIP GROUPS

'Adolescent groups show three main forms of social structure

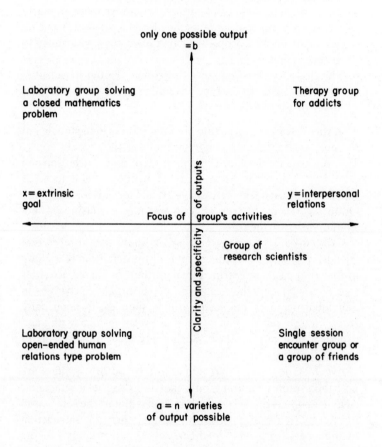

Figure 3   Location of a group of friends in relation to the dimensions xy
extrinsic goal/interpersonal relations and ab diffuse unspecified
single/specific goal

Source: Gahagan (1975).

which have been discussed – informal hierarchy, sociometric structure and norms – but in special ways.'

(Argyle 1969 : 247)

Bales (1955) noted that as groups developed they tended to shift from a task- to a friendship orientation. This was a clear vindication that relationships in a group had to be brought to a level of friendship before members could adequately proceed with the task. The nature of purely friendship groups is to substitute the achievement and maintenance of good, satisfying, socio-emotional relationships for the task. In other words, the task of friendship groups is to generate and hold onto satisfying relationships. As all task-oriented groups have to cope with socio-emotional factors at some level, what we can learn about the process from successful friendship groups should be directly applicable to created groups in handling this particular problem.

Most of the material so far produced about friendship groups tends to be about adolescent groups probably because, as Fraser (1978) says, they 'are most common during adolescence'. Button (1974) found that if young people were 'not adequately contained in their friendships' they were often in greater trouble than their peers who were. He also indicated that although the pattern of friendship remained similar, the people who occupied the role of friend could change. This leads to an assumption that the structural nature of friendship groups is perhaps the most important factor. Translated in group terms this means that membership, that is, acceptance, is crucial and the group as an entity in its own right is of greater salience than the individual members as people.

Button puts forward an interesting comparison of what he calls the levels of companionship – these were readily recognized by the young people themselves as representing different states. They are:

1 *Close friend* – defined as 'someone you like and probably most frequently whom you trust and rely on, to whom you tell secrets – and expect him or her to do the same to you'.
2 *Other friend* – someone you like and possibly meet frequent-

ly, whose company you seek, and who is more than an
associate but not a close friend.

3   *Associate* – you may not go out of your way to meet this
person, but if they happened to be about you would join up
with them.

4   *Aquaintance* – someone you would acknowledge upon meeting but would not normally choose as a companion for a social
occasion.

Friendship groups would therefore seem to consist of people who
would admit to having level 1 and 2 relationships with most of
the other members, that is, the bond is close friend or other
friend. Obviously in any large group there will be members who
are bonded to very few others in the group and they will tend to
be the more peripheral members of the group.

   Friendship groups are peer groups. They are supportive and
are often very confining; but they also provide a high level of
satisfaction for their members. The latter is related to security, to
the ability to predict responses, and to the fact of acceptance.
Often these factors are enhanced in the level of apparent satisfaction they offer by comparison with other previous groups, the
family, for example. Without doubt, friendship groups act as
reference groups for most of their members in the sense that clear
levels of approval/disapproval are available to cover a wide range
of conduct, attitudes, and beliefs. Many people who will not
accept an authoritarian declaration of the correctness or otherwise of behaviour will conform to the norms of behaviour of their
friendship group even when there is no possibility that the group
would ever be able to detect deviance.

   Thus, friendship groups offer acceptance, credibility, and an
identity to their members, as well as affection and other forms of
support. It is interesting that the strongest and the most numerous friendship groups are found during adolescence when, in
fact, the problems of maturation are precisely those that friendship groups seem so well disposed to meet.

GROUP PROCESSES THAT FOSTER FRIENDSHIP AND
THOSE THAT MAY NOT

'Another difficulty in studying real groups stems from the experimenter's usual lack of knowledge of the past history of the group. In a typical existing group the members have developed a shorthand language through their shared experiences which permits them to refer to complex issues in terms foreign to the outside observer.' (Hoffman 1965 : 127)

Interaction

Perhaps the chief activity of friendship groups is interaction and this leads such groups to the distinction of being the only naturally occurring groups that continually monitor and study their own interaction. In the group, relationships are co-operative rather than conflicting, and are based upon physical attractiveness, sharing, and frequency of contact. The group has common goals largely to do with the satisfaction of social drives; physical proximity tends to generate increased interactions that are mutually rewarding and thus decrease the cost of membership. Though often of an unstable nature, positive feedback and support are factors of friendship groups. Most members of such a group are personally compatible, as liking and wanting-to-be-with are the prime attraction to joining such a group. There are some similarities and some interesting contrasts with the family group in the kind of bonds created. For example, friendship groups frequently become the preferred alternative to the family group and give support to the younger family member trying to break from the family to establish his or her independence. Of course, this situation must generate a great sense of obligation to the friendship group thus increasing the level of conformity to its requirements. It is significant that most friendship groups occur during adolescence when the need for support, identity, and affection may well be at its highest and that later in life such groups are much less frequent and tend to have a different character, being work based or founded in common interests, for example.

Development

Friendship groups show little of the classic development of other groups. They are characterized by an easy intimacy and accept-ance. The main reason for this apparent lack of developmental stages may not be too difficult to discover. Most groups of strangers go through a fairly long period of about twelve hours of contact before the members have sufficient experience of each other to be able to predict with reasonable accuracy the likely responses to their behaviour. In other words, some level of trust will develop. It also takes some time to find out what sort and what degree of satisfactions the groups can mediate for the individual and at what cost. Friendship groups start with liking and a fairly clear idea of what the group has to offer. Thus, if we take the simple formula of group development postulated by Schutz (1959) – $ICA(IC\ A\ .\ .\ .)^n\ AC\ I$ (where A = affection, C = control, and I = inclusion), friendship groups start at the level of affection. As this is the major objective of the group's existence, development to further stages is not a priority.

Structure

Friendship groups have a role structure formed by a linkage of affective bonds. The nature of the group's structure makes members very conscious of its inclusive qualities and of their different relationships to non-members even though the mem-bership may be constantly changing, which, incidentally, is another factor that reduces the need for group development. Members are usually of the same sex and form a peer relationship structure that often has an individual locked into a fixed role from which it is exceedingly difficult to escape. Despite the informal hierarchy in such groups, it seems to be that a member's cost for membership is to perform continually the role to which he or she has been allocated. This again mitigates against group develop-ment but it does offer the security and predictability that under-lie the group's reason for existence.

Sub-groups

Sub-groups, usually based upon similarity and proximity, form and change within the larger structure. But as friendship groups are never very large, the number of sub-groups and their influence is equally small.

Goals

The overriding goal of the friendship group is likely to be the maintenance of the group and the well-being of the members, that is, to continue to meet as a group, to indulge in joint activities, and thus to increase the social interaction. The group may have other short-term goals, for example in terms of their joint activities. The main need of the group is to provide enjoyment and pleasure in each other's company, and other goal achievements are not really important. Many kinds of output will facilitate the development of the desired affective relationship. Friendship groups evolve their own norms for regulating acceptance and subsequent behaviour that may not revolve round a set of roles. There will almost certainly be a strong normative influence, developing what Button (1974) calls a 'ball and chain' group, about clothes and appearance that identify individuals as members. As has been mentioned, the level of uniformity is very high and is willingly offered because the group is important in interpersonal matters and group activities that confirm the shared values and opinions. Most of the group's norms are tacit and the sanctions applied on their breach understood and, once again, the speed of their production is due to pre-existing friendships and to the esteem and affection that group members already have for each other.

Cohesion

Cohesion of friendship groups is very strong. The sense of being a part of a system that supports the individual supplies some very urgent needs of identity, for confirmation is all-enveloping. The group stands united against common enemies and common uncertainties and offers high levels of satisfaction, an incredibly potent combination for the development of group solidarity. Thus, the *influence* of the group is equally high. By producing a set of self-definitions for members, by demonstrating that failure to comply will be met with rejection, when acceptance is the most important need of members, the group can offer such high levels of satisfaction that the pressure it can exert is considerable. The *climate* that is generated is thus supportive and cohesive and offers security.

The actual physical *environment* may dictate who makes friends with whom and also reinforces selection once made. In general, environment shapes the membership of friendship groups in terms of propinquity and proximity. Few friendships survive removal to a geographically distant location; members are much more likely to join a group within their new area.

Membership

Membership is so much influenced by factors of similarity, for instance in relation to ethnic origin, socio-economic background, religion, and education, that one is compelled to say that the main criterion for selection to a friendship group is the liking we have for people who agree with us. Common interests and attitudes, familiarity, and equality are all factors of similarity. That members of friendship groups tend to judge others in the group to be more like themselves than they really are, indicates the enormous value placed upon similarity. Even complementarity seems to be a less firm basis for friendship than similarity.

Time

Time does not have a great role to play as a constraint in this kind of group. Changes in relationship occur over time, but the group's main function is only weakly time-related. Likewise, the *size* of such groups is small and limited, as is their *open* nature, by the admission criterion of liking. However, the group is a 'core' group with a changing membership but with effective transfer of culture through the core.

Activity

The main activity of friendship groups is just 'being together' and all other activities subscribe to this one. Social interaction is important and there is often much bodily contact through games and ritual procedures. *Leaders* seem often to be chosen for particular activities, which is in line with members being locked into particular roles. Leadership is often related to the perception of members of the competence of the person chosen. In fact, the whole question of leadership in friendship groups is unusually charismatic because otherwise there is some necessary conflict between friendship and the exercise of authority. Charisma is necessary in the leader because friends are associations of equals; authority, the exercise of power not underwritten by liking, would tend to destroy the foundations of group attraction.

Selection

On closer examination, selection reveals some fascinating aspects that are much more subtle than straight liking or location. Individuals joining a friendship group are seeking reassurance on the one hand and stimulation on the other, two factors that would seem to indicate almost opposing predictions as to the choices that would be made. The bases of the judgement seem to be dependent upon individual characteristics and viewpoint, but perception of the quality of status, of similar moral outlooks, and of similar standards tends to play a large part in selection. The group knows that its environmental constraints mean that an expectation of similar social conditions is valid, but admission to an existing friendship group seems to be dependent upon the applicant's being able to establish his or her similarity to the existing members and also their worth in terms of the group's standards.

There is no explicit *contract* as far as becoming a member of a friendship group is concerned, but there is always a clear understanding that liking and similarity are the main criteria of acceptance. Once in the group, the concept of loyalty becomes important and it is these three factors that constitute the main reasons for leaving the group or being rejected by it.

If liking changes, if a member becomes significantly dissimilar to the other group members, or if he or she demonstrates clear disloyalty, then there is no place for that person in the group. Inevitably such things happen to all members. Members change as they grow older, their needs change or can be met more effectively from some other source; the attractiveness of the group diminishes as its ability to reward decreases; other people or other groups become more important and loyalty is transferred. But, being an open group, as members opt out at one end others tend to come in at the other. Like the family, the bonds generated in a friendship group may well be long-lasting even though contact is never re-established, probably because the relationships were based upon affection, need, and shared experience, and were often highly rewarding.

SUMMARY

This chapter has been concerned with the analysis of friendship groups in terms of the 'factors-affecting'. Such groups have been shown to be most common among adolescents when affiliative and identity needs are at their strongest. Clearly friendship groups have a peculiar character essentially designed to meet these needs. Thus, they are founded on affection and similarity. They have strong bonds of loyalty and show little development over time as development is not a necessary factor in the production of rewards for their members. Normative pressures are high because levels of satisfaction are also very high. Membership depends upon clear criteria, all of which have similarity as a fundamental aspect. The groups are open though with a core to transmit group culture and their emotional effect is often long-lasting, certainly outliving actual membership of the group.

Characteristically, friendship groups are the clearest of natural indicators of the effect of selective design. Because liking is a major criterion for selection, development starts part of the way through the possible sequence and soon stops; because members are well rewarded for membership, group influence operates at a very high level; because the needs that the group satisfies tend to be transient, the group is open, and so on. The friendship group meets the needs of its members and is clearly very limited in its scope by this fact. But what it does do, it does very well, using its selected resources with efficiency.

6

WORK ORGANIZATIONS

'the last hundred years have seen not only the dehumanising of manual work, with the introduction of mass-production methods and "scientific management", and a consequent reduction in the satisfaction which an individual can derive from the performance of a skilled craft, but also universal acceptance of the idea that everyone *ought* to work even though they may have no absolute economic necessity to do so.'

(Nicholson 1977 : 75)

The whole area of study of work organizations is fraught with complications. Economists have often been accused of simplifying their analysis by ignoring any psychological concepts of the human beings involved in favour of consideration of the work-force as a cost or a productive unit. Management techniques tend to have been concerned with efficiency, production figures, and the development of methods that can coax and persuade the work-force to achieve the kind of targets required.

The rational economic man of the economists does not exist and, in fact, never has existed. Moreover, the concept of a work organization as a complex machine for turning out goods and services that just happens to contain human beings as an essential ingredient is equally fallacious. However, the analysis of work organizations is a valid procedure whatever the basis upon which the organizations are founded. It is possible that such an analysis would reveal strengths and weaknesses in any organization but the crunch point is that given the objectives of the organization, how can the facts of the analysis be used? Should they be used to improve the performance of the existing organization in some way, or should they be used to restructure the whole process, or parts of the process, or should they be ignored?

One of the salient objectives of this book has been to demonstrate that whether or not people take notice of group processes and the other affecting factors in group situations, these factors do influence the outcome of group situations and often produce results that in either direction, intensity, or nature have not been allowed for in the calculations of the planners. These kinds of consequence are frequently put down to 'human nature', a statement that is true enough but that tends to be used dismissively and consequently gets planners nowhere.

While it has long been recognized that boring and repetitive jobs give little or no job satisfaction to the people who work at them, the only alternative satisfaction that has received much serious consideration has been the money-reward. Cash-in-hand to buy the materials and services outside the place of work, that provide a level of satisfaction, has been agreed by all sides of industry to be one of the balancing factors, although some attention has been paid to work conditions and the kind of facilities available to workers.

The 1939 Hawthorne Experiment (Roethlisberger and Dickson 1939), and others since, have called into question the absolute value of changes in conditions and have shown that other factors often enough unheeded at the time tended to influence how the changes were accepted by the work-force. Two of the main factors in this sphere of influence seem to have been the cohesive nature of the work groups and whether that cohesion was a bond against management decisions or was in tune with them. Of course, other outside factors are involved, such as the level of unemployment, states of war, recession, and boom.

What adds up to 'satisfaction' in work organizations is a complex of factors. One thing is certain, however. Members of any organization are a great deal more influenced in the decisions they make and the actions they take by what they perceive as 'satisfactions' than by the large-scale objectives of the organization itself.

The amount of investigation of the effect that groups within an organizational structure can have on its performance is quite small. What is presented here is a synthesis of some of the available material.

WORK ORGANIZATIONS AS STRUCTURES CONTAINING GROUPS

'One of the central features of work is that it is usually done in groups, groups of individuals cooperating under the direction of a leader or leaders.'   (Argyle 1972 : 104)

All large organizations tend to have grown from small groups and recognition of the fact that within any such organizations, small groups exist, has long been with us. Indeed, recognition of the discrepancies between the formal and informal structure of an organization has also been clear for a long time. But recognition of the informal system has not been accompanied by the realization that for many people within an organization the informal group is more 'real' than the formal system, that it often has different goals and thus works in significantly different directions to the avowed and official aims of the organization.

Due to the development of Organizational Development programmes, we have become much more aware that any large organization, and smaller ones to a lesser degree, can contain individuals and small groups who, while believing that what they are doing is largely compatible with the formal aims of the organization, are, in fact, moving in more or less contrary directions to those aims. Moreover, individual or small group perceptions of the organizational behaviour of other individuals and small groups is often grossly at odds with the way in which those same individuals and small groups would describe what they were doing and how they believed they were perceived by others.

There are limits to the number of relationships of more than a casual nature any one person can have, or wishes to make, in a period of time. All large groups must therefore be constellations of smaller groupings, some of which are more or less permanent and some of which are essentially transient, supplying momentary and changing needs. No one seems to be sure about the limits of relationship making and difficulties lie in the fact that number and intensity may be exchangeable values so that a smaller number of intense contacts may equate in terms of satisfaction with a much larger number of more superficial contacts.

One thing is certain, however. The immediacy and supportive nature of these small group contacts must make them much more a reality than the socially distant organization of which they are a part. It must allow for a very clear appreciation of the inclusive/exclusive nature of group membership. All the factors that generate acceptance of some people as members of any particular group are exactly the factors that exclude others.

The simple fact of contact carries with it the possibility of balancing liking and appreciation of others. Liking is a salient factor both in group formation and in the acceptance of a standard or normative behaviour supported by group pressure. Shared experience, that is, experience which is common, not just similar, is also a bonding factor and tends to generate a sense of common understanding. With such shared experience individuals have evidence that others have similar knowledge of 'what it is like' and thus a knowledgeable and experiential understanding that is not shared by those who have not gone through the experience.

Where the tasks in an organization are diverse then the basis for a number of 'shared experience' groupings is equally large. What is more, the interests of such groupings may well be not entirely consonant with the formal aims of the organization as a whole and often enough may be in direct conflict with them. For example, there may be a primary desire to see that no one is put upon rather than to ensure the highest possible standard of production.

Given that large organizations have increasing problems in communication, the formation and enduring existence of many small groupings must often ensure that communication problems are further exacerbated. Different groupings within a large organization seldom realize the extent to which their group identity tends to preclude any common understanding. Indeed, it is the function of group norms not only to ensure conformity within the group but also to highlight the difference of behaviour and belief in other groups. Often enough belonging to one group endows members with acceptable attitudes towards other groups with sanctions imposed for those who show any inclination to attempt increased understanding of members of the outgroup. The obvious common factors seem to be easily obliterated by group-supported differences.

Interestingly enough, the strength of such conditioned perceptions is resistive to rational argument but not so impregnable to experience. However, most organizational structures created round division of labour and specialization do not offer the opportunity for experiencing the roles of others, and thus the much less effective tool of rational argument is all that is left to bridge some very wide gaps in understanding.

THE PROBABLE EFFECTS OF GROUP PROCESSES IN WORK GROUPS IN THE LIGHT OF THE DECLARED OBJECTIVES OF THE CONTAINING ORGANIZATION

'C. I. Barnard has pointed out that all large organisations may be thought of as having been built up from a number of smaller groups. These small groups vary in size but average about eight or ten people, the number being determined by the fact that problems of communication become greater as the size of the group increases.'   (Brown 1954 : 124)

The dynamics of the small groups within a large organization are an enduring function of that organization, affecting its performance in one way or another. While all the processes and constraints are constantly operating, information is available on the effects of only some of them. But even in this partial state of knowledge it is obvious what powerful affecting factors they can be.

Cohesiveness

Cohesiveness, which has been defined as the attractiveness of the group for its members, the liking, and the sense of belonging, and the bond that creates the sense of being a unit, has some very powerful effects in the work group situation. As most work groups are dependent upon a degree of co-operation from their members it is not surprising to find that cohesive groups are somewhat more productive than non-cohesive groups. Basically this is because interaction between members is maintained at a high level with the consequences of smoother and more effective communication, making work a more pleasurable experience for those engaged in it. Of course, the interaction levels can become so high that the main objective of the group becomes social and production is relegated to a secondary role. The spin-offs from the increase of satisfaction in the work situation may include a reduction in days lost through absenteeism, a reduction in tension and friction between workers in the group, and an increase in group-approved behaviour.

Of course, cohesiveness in a work group can produce effects that are not positively related to the organizational aims. New members to such a group find their position dependent upon acceptance. If they cannot get this acceptance this usually means that they are stressed to the point of leaving. A further factor lies in the way in which cohesiveness enhances exclusivity of membership to the obvious detriment of other groups and their members, which will often result in competitive attitudes and sometimes in lack of co-operation.

Cohesion

Cohesion cannot develop well where members of groups are separated by physical space and have only a limited opportunity to interact. Such workers are more likely to belong to groups outside the isolating influence of the workplace. Cohesion is strengthened by time spent together, by group members being similar in status, age, background, and ideas, by shared incentive in which each member realizes that he or she is of great value to the group in achieving its aims, and by groups that are small enough for members to know and appreciate each other as members. Other factors which tend to develop cohesion are the social skills and integrating force of leadership acts. The role models set by influential group members and any threat that menaces the whole group, providing they have been long enough together to operate as a unit in response to it, also tend to develop cohesion.

Norms

The norms of a group are the often unwritten rules by which the group operates and which serve to maintain its unique identity. In work situations norms create standards. So, for example, how hard a person works is not gauged by what he or she wants to earn, nor by the demands set by the organization, but by the agreement of the work group as to what is fair and equitable considering the abilities, skills, and needs of the total group membership. Safety regulations are often ignored because the work group's attitude to them is derisory. Group pressure can ensure that all members conform to that attitude even though their individual response would have been to abide by the regulations. Tradition has often ignored and rejected innovation because of just such a need to be accepted by a work group.

The approved way of doing things covers output, attitudes to others in the organization, social activities, language, the way people dress, even the jokes they tell, and almost every other factor of the work scene. These tend to make groups that stay together for long periods rather conservative in attitude and behaviour and somewhat resistant to change.

Norms do not have to be restrictive and where they set high levels of achievement they may well square with the aims of the organization. So much is this so, that groups are now often formed around experienced people whose routine behaviour enshrines organizationally acceptable norms. Thus, a group forms around a role model and develops the standards held by the nuclear person. This is not an easy situation because lower standards are often easier to maintain and less demanding of effort. In any case, there is a tendency for systems to run down without the injection of new energy, so increases in organizationally acceptable normative behaviour tend to be hard to maintain.

Something has already been said about the process of decision making from the point of view of the individual who participates in it. It is worth repeating that decisions that affect an individual's existence, and that are made where the individual has no influence, constitute one of the clearest indications of the power relationships that exist in that situation. Individuals often seek to alleviate their powerlessness by action in combination and by large-scale actions that are often out of proportion to the presenting cause because the action is compounded of thousands of different cases of individual grievances. Action in combination allows the feeling of overwhelming power, the exercise of which certainly gives some compensation for the powerlessness experienced in other situations.

All the group processes are fundamentally based on interaction. Without interaction there can be no group. Thus isolation brought about by physical distance or overwhelming noise inhibits interaction in the workplace. While the work units are made up of individuals in the place of work, conditions in the canteen or recreation facilities may be more conducive to group formation.

Interaction

Interaction by members of a group develops a supportive structure over time. Members gain acceptance for their views, receive emotional and physical support when work is exhausting, dangerous, or productive of stress, and also acquire a sense of belonging. It is indicative of the power assigned to interaction and group acceptance that the universal sanction for misbehaviour is exclusion and isolation. A total verbal barrier inhibiting interaction is a mark of high disapproval.

A factor that greatly affects interaction levels is the size of the group. Large groups tend to split into smaller groups but all the evidence points to the fact that small groups produce more satisfying working conditions, judged on the bases of production and the figures of absenteeism.

No work group is composed of totally disengaged human beings. But often enough work schedules seem to be planned as if this were so. An appreciation of the dynamics of any group situation offers the possibility of choice between various methods of change and between more and less acceptable demands. The nature of any particular work group has already set some boundaries to what it can be expected to achieve. This does not imply that it cannot achieve other levels of operation; it does mean that the current state of its operational dynamics has to be an important factor in the change approach. It may well be that changes in level of operation can only be achieved as and when changes in the dynamic structure have been brought about.

A common industrial complaint has often been lack of consultation. As we have seen, members' involvement in decisions that affect the group tends to increase their commitment to the decisions that they arrive at. But involvement means involvement, an active participation resulting in a sense of being part of the decision-making process. Having some influence on the outcome is what actually generates commitment and not some superficial request for agreement to a scheme that is already fully contrived. Such consultation gives the strongest of non-verbal communications about where the source of power lies in spite of what may be said to the contrary. The feeling such situations generate is one of powerlessness to influence outcomes that directly concern the individual's existence.

More attention to the design factors that enhance the group dynamics positively related to the organization's aims would ensure increases in productivity. Too often changes are created because fashions change, because new ideas for saving this or that are abroad, or because change in aims or organizational structure are necessitated by administrative factors. None of this can be ignored. But what is seen as necessity in one part of an organization may well be seen as totally destructive of a method of existence in another, and the response may be overtly aggressive and defensive.

Thus, while positive use has been made of group dynamics from the management's view of the organization (that is, to increase productivity), little use has been made by either side of such knowledge to increase the possibility of working together at all levels of an organization. Management are often enough concerned that management levels shall not waste valuable time, energy, and creativeness by pulling in opposite directions (see, for example, Golembiewski 1980; Bennis 1966; and Margulies and Raia 1979). Consequently an understanding of group dynamics and of human relationships has generated a multi-million dollar personal-growth industry in the United States.

In this country the growth of such learning and experiential opportunities has neither been so great nor so fast. But it has been even more one-sided in that work-forces in industry and business have tended to see their best interest being guarded by traditional trade union activities and this has resulted in the continued development of entrenched positions. Only few courses in group and committee skills and negotiating patterns have ever been provided for workers. The organization of industry and commerce is again held to be political and related to the class system. In fact, so much is this true that knowledge of group dynamics is often rejected on the basis that it is an apolitical approach and thus does not get to the root cause of the conflict. In one sense this accusation is true because the history of group dynamic knowledge in organizations, short though it is, has almost always come from the management levels. It is seen, therefore, as a tool of management in much the same way as the early time and motion studies were regarded. What we are faced with here is the rejection of group dynamic analysis on the basis of its possible use. Of course, this does not preclude understanding of work groups in the terms of group dynamics, but it does clearly indicate why the most prominently available data about such groups clusters so heavily around all the processes that are closely connected with ingroup protective behaviour such as cohesion, norms, standards, values, climate, and all the constraints that clearly signal the need for such protective behaviour.

So successful is this behavioural balance that new approaches stand little chance of success as the difference of such situations is regarded with suspicion from either side, and inevitably the existing attitudes predispose the perception of all to overlook the possible advantages. At a guess, I would say that only change of almost tragic proportions will tend to break this kind of stalemate, and even the few examples where change has been brought about by rational means are not sufficient evidence that this has become widespread practice.

SUMMARY

Work organizations are structures that contain groups, but those groups are much less salient to the organization than the 'group' concept is to the family or the collection of friends. One major reason for this is that in any large organization identifiable groups proliferate, and thus each is likely to be rather less essential to the continuance of the whole. Work groups have more of the characteristics of sub-groups than of groups in their own right. Yet this may be a false analogy as all groups are embedded in a supra-structure and contain component entities within themselves.

Certain elements of group dynamics can be shown to facilitate production work and equally others can be shown to inhibit it. The whole analysis of group behaviour is inextricably bound up in the business of goals. Work and management groups within the same organization may have diametrically opposed goals. This may be so despite an almost total lack of recognition on either side that such a situation exists. Organization Development analysis often reveals disparate groups in one organization operating in counterproductive ways while implicitly believing that they are working to achieve the same ends.

Much of this kind of conflict is due to other groups, reference groups that have generated standards of judgement of situations based on different criteria. Thus, while it is possible to show that work groups use selected group dynamics to become efficiently functioning units, and while aims within the larger organization are overtly or covertly disparate, it is equally true that selective dynamics ensure conflict by the efficient following of aims and equally efficient rejection of the assumed aims of other groups. Some may argue that such conflict is inevitable in a society already full of conflict, but the fact remains that where aims overlap, where a consensus of aims is possible, then the reduction in the use of conflict dynamics releases considerable energy for mutually agreed productive ends.

7

TEAMS

INTRODUCTION

'Team – set of players forming a side in a football match or other game or sport; set of persons working together.'
(Concise Oxford Dictionary)

Perhaps the most interesting word in the dictionary definition of 'team' is the word 'set'. By implication a 'set' of people or pieces suggests a definite number, each member or part of which bears a clear and observable relationship to each other and to the set as a whole. In this way the pieces of a chess 'set' have defined roles within the overall aim of beating an opposing set. However skilful the set-director (in this case the player) may be, the moves of the pieces conform to an exact pattern and it is within the limits imposed by these patterns that the director must work. All teams partake of this rather structured nature and it is this that largely distinguishes teams from any other form of grouping.

Teams are co-operative groups in that they are called into being to perform a task or tasks that cannot be attempted by an individual. In this sense all groups are teams but the organization that constitutes a team is not one generally found in other forms of group. Thus, if a team is a particular kind of group organization that has arisen in order to meet certain kinds of social requirement, then an analysis of what a team does and the organization it has developed to do it should reveal the dynamics relevant to this kind of task. Not only should this indicate methods of creating more effective teams, but it should also show the clear-cut cause/effect ratio of assembling in one grouping of certain group processes at given intensities.

Given the fact that teams must have occurred very early in our history as a method of dealing with certain situations, it is somewhat surprising to discover that judging by the amount of literature it has produced, the analysis of teams as a specific kind of social group does not seem to have aroused much interest. Most writers seem to indicate that the dynamics of teams are the dynamics of groups in general, which is true, and that the different emphases are not sufficiently different to warrant special mention, which is not true, at least in my estimation.

In a situation such as the formation of a national 'team' in some sport, it is interesting to note the reactions of selected members to the processes of selection and formation. Generally speaking, players are selected on the basis of their performance in a team of which they are a more or less permanent member; others are selected on their individual performance and become members of a loose collectivity, which is a team in name only. The former then have to perform in a group whose members are often unused to one another and who may have frequently been on opposing sides. The concept of team formation in use here is that a team comprises a series of specialists controlled by a leader, and that because the specialist roles are well understood, the parts should fit together in a functional whole.

That this does not gel with the personal experience of some of the special units involved can be gleaned from comments they make about 'settling down' over time and about having played together often enough to realize the complementary nature of the roles. In a word, they have practised not only their individual expertise but also their function as part of a unit containing discrete but dependent entities. Alternatively, a team leader has to know the units in his or her control so well that he or she can devise patterns for their deployment to meet most of the contingencies they will meet in play. The team response is then dependent upon the leader's recognition of the opportunity and instigation of the appropriate pattern and of the individual members' performing their ascribed role within that pattern more or less irrespective of individual assessment of the situation.

In either case, the team functions effectively only when its members operate as smoothly interlocking and complementary parts of the larger whole, eschewing much independent choice in favour of predictable behaviour. Familiarity would seem to lend added weight in that it would allow individuals the independence to take advantage of changes in the pattern of play by instigating sudden changes in their contribution to the team pattern. Familiarity would allow other members to recognize the change and adopt the new pattern based on their expectations from previous experience. This kind of behaviour contains all the essentials of a leadership act.

A team is a task-oriented group, its behaviour is constrained to eliminate actions that are not essential to task achievement. Its code of practice demands a high level of conformity and may even be condemnatory of successful independent actions unless they are 'planned in' to the team pattern. Some teams can, and do, develop 'star' patterns that specialize even further the functions of one or more players/members thereby creating an élite but dependent sub-group. Whatever way the pattern emerges, it has the essential nature of a disciplined package with strong sanctions available for contraventions of its overall unity of strategy.

THE NATURE OF A TEAM AND ITS PURPOSE

'Teams are groups of people who co-operate to carry out a joint task. They may be assigned to different work roles, or be allowed to sort them out between themselves and change jobs when they feel like it, for example the crews of ships and aircraft, research teams, maintenance gangs and groups of miners.' (Argyle 1972 : 110)

The co-operative and interpretive function of a team (see note p. 72) generates what has been called 'interdependent relationships' (Allen 1965), and all the available evidence points to the fact that interdependent relationships in a group allow greater pressure to be applied than in groups with a greater degree of independence among members. There is sufficient evidence from team sports that personal dislike is often set aside during a team performance because a greater level of satisfaction is accessible for all the team members in their combined achievement than can be gained in the expression of personal feelings.

The whole issue of competition enters here, as does the effect upon group cohesion of perception of being attacked by outsiders. As we shall see, the processes and factors affecting team behaviour demonstrate a clear recognition of the major purposes for which teams are created and serve to enhance functional effectiveness.

Interaction

As in all groups, interaction is fundamental to a team's existence, but again, as in all other groups, the level and nature of the interaction in a team has distinctive qualities. The nature of a team's identity in fact is dependent upon a high level of interaction being demonstrated. In other words, the appearance of interaction at a good level indicates to observers the cohesive teamlike quality of the group in its public performance. In actual fact, interaction in an effective team is usually devoted to establishing and maintaining reciprocal dependence and familiarity among members in areas associated with the team's performance. Dependence is almost a *sine qua non* for the existence of a team although it is often enough restricted to the actual public performance of the team, while familiarity is necessary to facilitate prediction and to enhance the sense of being a functional unit.

The meshing together of the functions of the different team members depends upon a clear act of subordination of rivalries with other members and of any egocentric behaviour. Take a team of trapeze artists, for example. Their lives rest on the absolute dependability of each other, and many exciting stories have been concocted around the intrusion of private aims into this essentially secure unit.

Development

This is not an essential feature of teams except in one highly specialized area, prediction. Given an amount of shared experience of operating as a team, the members may not, and often do not, develop an overall trust in each other that continues to exist outside the team performance as members of personal growth groups will. But in order to perform efficiently they must develop a reasonable level of security based on the ability to predict with higher than chance levels of accuracy the responses of other team members. Co-ordination, which is basic in team performance, tends to rely heavily on each member doing what is expected of him or her so that the whole effort blends and moves in the direction of the team's overall purpose.

Structure

The structure of teams is not primarily a constellation of persons but a fairly tightly knit relationship of roles. This structure has a large formal element; newcomers who are able to fill a particular team role elsewhere can slot into the structure immediately on arrival, though their team performance will tend to be more efficient once they have more shared experience and have been able to adjust expectations to the minimal idiosyncracies of the new team. In this way, status differences may not be too important, although particular team approaches can create a particular role, that of star performer, because this appears to be the best use of available resources, to achieve the group's aims. The interdependency (mentioned above) is, however, still maintained and still reciprocal. A 'star' system is clearly part of the role structure and as long as it obtains results will be accepted even to the glorification of the individual playing the 'star' role.

Sub-group formation

As would be expected, sub-group formation does not occur spontaneously but only as part of team design and must always remain subject to the overall pattern. A sub-group can only have a life of its own in so far as it enables the team to achieve its objectives.

Group goals

In most teams, group goals are very clear. In fact, teams are not only task or goal-oriented, but the design and co-operative nature of a team also arises from a perception that such a structure is the most effective way to achieve desired outcomes.

Decision making

Decision-making processes are thus rational and open to performance feedback that can than be used to modify design, tactics, and, ultimately, performance. Efficient teams have a self-reviewing mechanism built into their design that allows monitoring and review of performance with the aim of enhancing standards. Access to this reviewing system is democratic and often actively encouraged.

Norms, standards, and values

The norms, standards, and values of a team are of great importance. They embody the essential system, the ways in which members are permitted to behave during team performance. Knowledge of the rules ensures that standards are maintained, and the dependent state of the members is generated and used for team ends only and not exploited for individual gain. Differences are minimized, a party line is maintained and consensus and solidarity buttressed by a kind of professional etiquette. Behaviour, for the time of the group's performance, must conform to strict rules so that no individual member has to think of his or her own security or support needs to the detriment of devotion to the team task.

Cohesion

As mentioned earlier, cohesion is essential. A reciprocal dependence and familiarity are needed to generate security, because performance without such security becomes not only individualistic but haphazard and uncertain. Even when mistakes are made by team members, other members have to suppress the desire to punish or chide in the public eye. If they do not, the team's unified image is clearly seen to be falling apart and, in the eyes of possible competitors, much of its strength has thus been lost and its weaknesses can be exploited.

Influence

The influence of the team on its members is quite a simple one. Conformity is more likely to produce rewards for all, and the failure of one ensures the failure of all. Thus, the pressure to conform is enhanced by a unanimously strong desire to succeed on the part of all team members. It is also maintained by a system of sanctions, not least of which is well nigh complete disapproval.

Climate

Teams generate a climate of loyalty, which stems from the acceptance of dependence on others to achieve a desired outcome. There is something of the secret society about all successful teams. Members accept the skills and knowledge of other members as a common resource and the sense of sharing and shared experience, which distinguishes members from non-members, is high.

Environment

The control of its environment is important to a team. For sports teams the home ground with its familiarity and increased sense of place and of ease can often inspire a better performance than strange grounds. The acceptance of a base is common to all members of a team and is one of the features that distinguishes members from non-members.

Membership

Membership is a constraint with powerful implications. The factors that comprise this constraint, namely the qualities, abilities, background, experience, attitudes, and ambitions, of members are all extremely relevant. Each member of a team is assumed to have special knowledge and competence and their selection and continuing membership of the team is dependent upon such special skills and abilities, these being a necessary ingredient of the team as a whole. If the membership changes, say in order to produce a team designed to meet a perceived difference of task, then only members whose abilities conform to the new requirements will be retained. Conversely, the performance of a team is significantly related to the ability of the members to produce only those activities that are in the interests of team efficiency. Thus, the ability to limit non-essential behaviours is almost as important as being able to produce those behaviours that brought about selection in the first place.

Along with functional roles, members of a team also perform ceremonial and ritual roles that act as a form of window-dressing and create a public image that enhances or attracts public support for their performance, whether this be as audience or as financial backers.

Time

Time is not unduly important as a constraint upon a team. It may be crucially important for individual members in the development of their personal skills and techniques, but if the design of a team has been well served by the selection of its members for their contribution, then only minimal time is required for such a team to be functionally effective. Time spent working together obviously increases the familiarity with response patterns, and, without doubt, as all of each member's potential cannot be known in advance, nor are their performances necessarily stable in terms of quality, more time can bring an increased knowledge and a more realistic level of expectation.

Resources

Such a concept leads straight into a consideration of resources. The skills members possess, their knowledge and abilities are the main resources a team possesses. This lays great emphasis on selection so that the total team is neither short of human resources nor forced to carry relatively unproductive components. Other resources of the material kind have obviously varying degrees of importance. In some cases they are essential. If the team is operating complex equipment, then the team's performance is largely dependent upon the efficiency of that equipment. Where a team's function is the exploitation of human abilities with only minimal equipment then the major resource is the human potential.

Size

Size is an important factor. Most teams are essentially small groups. Beyond twelve to fifteen members, the kind of structure I have been describing, is very hard to maintain. The multiplying of roles, the increased potential of relationships and ideas, and the increased possibility of individuals opting out, bring about diminishing returns unless an increase in rigidity and regulatory procedures accompanies the increase in size. This may also bring about a decrease in achievement levels because performance will necessarily be restricted in a creative sense by the growth of restrictive discipline. This is an area where the degree and nature of discipline has to be appropriate to the task the team was created to perform. It is noteworthy that essentially creative functions seem to be mainly related to individual performance and not to the work of teams.

Teams are essentially *open groups* but with a strong tendency for the membership to remain static for long periods of time. Most teams are formed from a collection of possible members and the nature of the team as a group of selected human components performing a well-defined task implies that modification, reselection, disbandment, and substitution are all possible in order to meet changed conditions. Thus, any team tends to be embedded in a larger group, all the members of which have the potential and possibility of being members of the team at any time. Sometimes this larger group may be just a list of names in the designer's records and the members may have little or no knowledge of each other's existence. Often the supply group is a very apparent reserve, clearly involved with the current team and often considered to be not only a reservoir but also a training group and an essential part of the team.

Activity

The activity of a team is always clearly defined. The team's task not only delineates the selection of team members but also the activities they will pursue in achieving group goals. As most teams are in competition with other similar teams, or with their recorded performance, agreement about activity is very necessary as efficiency in performance is a high-level, proximate goal of any team.

Leadership acts

Leadership acts in teams possess some very interesting qualities. Conflict often arises between the team leader in his or her leadership function and the team leader as a member, so much so, that many teams prefer to keep the two functions quite separate. Where these separate roles occur, the team leader has some very distinctive functions. He or she:

1 May be responsible for selection.
2 Is responsible for ensuring that the discipline of the team produces the high level of performance and interdependence a team needs.
3 Is responsible for the allocation of roles and the use of resources.
4 Decides upon the team strategy and plans its policies.
5 Assumes a greater degree of responsibility to the team's audience or others concerned with its performance.
6 Makes considerable demands upon team members.

A team leader bears a responsibility to ensure success and thus leadership always has a strong directive element. This is true when the team leader is also a participating member of the team and this highlights an essential role conflict between directive leader and the co-operative normative behaviour of a member. This conflict has often been demonstrated where members of high performance have been given the role of leader and their performance has declined as they find that occupying two very dissimilar roles simultaneously is too demanding.

Selection

Selection has already been mentioned as a crucial factor in a team and all that needs to be said here is that once the level of skill has been taken into account, selection must create team members who can trust each other to perform correctly and who will not be indiscreet in their team-related behaviour. Such behaviour is stipulated in their *contract*, an agreement to which team members subscribe. It is an agreement to behave scrupulously within team norms and to maintain the team standards.

The analogy of a team with a machine composed of smoothly interlocking parts is sometimes made for obvious reasons. Team design is the most efficient way that human beings have discovered of providing a short- or limited-duration performance at high levels of intensity with maximum effectiveness. This implies that (a) the level of design and selection is of a very high order; (b) the human occupant of the team role is less significant qua human being than his or her ability to perform his or her allotted role; (c) in lieu of normal social interaction the relationship of the role occupants will be strictly governed by a unanimously accepted set of rules; and, finally, (d) leadership will be precisely located and directive in nature.

These are all factors that eliminate much of the time needed for growing together; development is assured by providing guidelines based on the assumption that such high levels of satisfaction will accrue from conformity and the huge amount of control needed by the members to achieve it will be seen as a worthwhile cost. Sometimes this assumption is incorrect. Other satisfactions appear more rewarding and the essential nature of 'teamness' is destroyed or reduced.

THE PROBABLE EFFECTS OF GROUP PROCESSES ON
TEAM PERFORMANCE

'Whether the members of a team stage similar individual performances or stage dissimilar performances which fit together into a whole, an emergent team impression arises which can be conveniently treated as a fact located between the individual performance on one hand and the total interaction of participants on the other.'   (Goffman 1969b : 85)

Steiner (1974), quoting the work of Torrance, showed that status differences in air crews presented with a problem affected the solutions produced in that whether right or wrong, the answers proffered by the high-status members were accepted by the low-status members of the crew. Low-status members with the right solution were unable to convince their fellow crew members of the rightness of their opinion in the face of the different opinions held by the high-status members. When men from different aircrews were formed into a problem-solving group, then who-ever had the correct solution, whether of high or low status, was much more able to convince others and affect the group outcome. Steiner comments that deviant opinions could be visited with reprisal in the whole crew groups whereas this was not likely to occur in the groups composed of members of several different crews. Steiner is suggesting that fear for their future well-being made low-status crew members accept what they may have known to be wrong.

There is another possibility. Crews are teams in which the safety of all is dependent upon each and every member exercising their allotted function in harmony with all the others and without fear or favour. Most team members are well aware that disagreement, even on matters with no direct reference to the team's existence, can impair their ability to function effectively within it. This interdependent state makes those involved very vulnerable to any decrease in loyalty on the part of any one of them. Thus, the relationship among Torrance's aircrews, which was an essential factor in the performance of their task, spil-led over into a task that was unrelated to their professional duties.

Many exciting stories have been written on this theme where disagreement between members of a team performing a danger-ous task (e.g. trapeze artists) has destroyed the necessary loyalty of the members to each other because strong motives of vengeance have occurred. This highlights the fact that the operating strength of a team is based upon a dependent trust and that this can easily become the source of its easy destruction by a sufficient change of attitude on the part of one or more members, especially when this change is successfully hidden from the others.

However, what appears to be a more important element in team design is the need to build in success. As mentioned earlier, the analysis of the factors affecting team design shows a heavy concentration on elements that first ensure as far as possible the smooth functioning of the team, second, eliminate unnecessary, delaying, or obstructive behaviour patterns and, third, maximize the potential of the group over a given period of time and allow for changes to meet changed circumstances. Thus competition, which seems to be the milieu in which most teams exist, ensures a concentration on factors producing maximum effectiveness with the resources available. In this sense what is missing from effective teams is as instructive in any analysis of group design as what is included.

If we take as an example of a team a group of workers in a Child Assessment and Treatment Unit working on behaviour modification lines, the elements of team design become apparent. In the first instance all those involved (specialists, parents, etc.) assess the situation as clearly as possible and come to a decision about what they will tackle and how. The first step is that all members are agreed on the team goals and the methods of achieving them. Then all those involved agree that they will adhere to the proposed schedule of treatment without variance for a given period. Change in the schedule can only be brought about by an agreement by all those involved to institute change and never by isolated action on the part of any member of the team. The essence of solidarity, which is extremely formidable in shaping the patient's view of the world in which he or she lives, is thus maintained. Cracks in this appearance of solidarity and unanimity are disastrous because they provide an alternative that is not required.

The maintenance of solidarity comes about through constant self-reviewing. Feedback to and from all team members constantly ensures that their construing of the situation is similar at all times (or at least their agreed acceptance of a particular construction) so that experience that is not universally shared in actual fact is shared by discussion and consideration, a sharing by proxy. The unanimity and uniformity, which can be so handicapping in decision-making groups by smothering alternatives, is a basic essential of the loyalty, respect, and support that a team system uses. The sheer effect of numbers of people of reasonably high status all behaving in the same way and speaking with one voice is very impressive.

In a word, the element of successful team functioning is a contract, an agreement to behave in a pre-ordained way for a given period of time. The contract is founded upon the belief that this is the most effective method of achieving certain desired outcomes. It tends to be shattered by frequent experience of failure. Sometimes it is obfuscated by the satisfaction gained from other outcomes not clearly or originally included in the contract (e.g. just being together).

SUMMARY

In this chapter team behaviour is analysed and shown to be of a contractual nature. This implies that the overall goal of the team as a performing group is agreed beforehand, that the methods of reaching that goal are also agreed upon, and each member undertakes to fulfil their allotted role. The team outcome is held to be more important than the personal goals of members for the duration of the team's performance.

It is noteworthy that T-groups and personal growth groups also develop this kind of contract but not by a contractual agreement, more by monitored and guided experience over a period of time. Both have in common the element of success. Appropriate behaviour is imprinted because it produces adequate rewards. In the team, which is a special form of work group, because they do not function together for long periods of time, appropriate behaviour has to be worked out, allocated, and adhered to. The cardinal sin for any team member is to individualize performance, and gain success at the expense of team mates.

Unlike work groups in general, teams are often isolated units, even if attached to larger organizations. Their aims, because of their own need for contractual agreement, are usually specific and seen as such by the supra-system. A team is a unique example of a collection of individuals held in dynamic and functional relationship over brief periods of time by agreement to their mutual and combined benefit.

8

COMMITTEES

'The organizational requirement for group problem-solving rests primarily on two assumptions: 1. the information needed for most management decisions must come from a variety of sources whose functional interdependence requires its simultaneous consideration and evaluation by all concerned; and 2. the acceptance of such decisions by the persons affected is often more important than the objective quality of the decision, and acceptance is promoted by participation in decision-making.'   (Hoffman 1965 : 100)

When Hoffman made the statement quoted above, he was engaged in trying to isolate the factors that inhibit group problem solving and those that facilitate it. He was concerned with this problem because large organizations often require that a great part of their work is done by committees. Thus, the question of group problem solving in an effective manner is of paramount importance.

Hoffman put forward the idea that the information available at the time seemed to indicate that the removal of the inhibiting factors in group problem solving did not of itself promote effective action and that facilitating factors had to be brought into the action before a committee's resources could be effectively utilized. It could be expected that effective committees should therefore not only eliminate as many inhibiting factors as possible but should also demonstrate a very positive use of facilitating factors. Generally speaking, inhibiting factors are conditions that prevent, or significantly reduce, the group's ability to express ideas freely. Conversely, promoting factors are conditions that facilitate or maximize the existing resources of the group.

Committees are decision-making groups. They are formed to solve problems and to take advantage of the supposed benefit of using groups rather than individuals in the process of decision making (see Introduction to Part Two *Table 2*). If solutions to problems, that is, decisions, are required then from this table we could expect that committees would tend to be groups that would be designed to use the resources of members, produce more solutions than individuals, eliminate inferior ideas, make more risky decisions, allocate tasks and roles, and minimize the sense of responsibility for individual members, and so on. Does the evidence of committee procedure show that these group-effect elements are built into committees or not?

I have indicated that committees are decision-making and problem-solving groups. Thus, the factors that inhibit the process of problem solving should be excluded in committee design and those that promote problem solving should be essential features of such design. Inhibiting factors as defined by Hoffman are as follows:

1 Too ready agreement – this is detrimental to the solution of complex problems.

2 Over dominance by the majority – this suppresses minority expression and may thus never allow correct solutions to surface. These two factors are promoted by a lack of confidence in the members of the committee, by the fact that deviant viewpoints are held, by dependence upon those members seen as able, or knowledgeable, or experienced, and by generalizations from previous experience.

3 The feedback to the group is not rewarding enough to increase participation.

4 There is undue importance attached to certain members, usually those who talk most, and their choice of solution is often accepted whatever its merits. The charisma and status

of such influential members is often related to the perception
that they are highly motivated.

5   The structure of the decision-making group may be an
     important inhibiting factor. For example the larger the group
     the more restrained its inhibited members tend to become
     and the influence of the confident members increases dis-
     proportionately. Or, if the structure is informal, this in-
     creases the influence of personality factors; power structures
     enhance the inhibiting effects of authority figures.
6   No organizational structure exists that can help to free the
     committee to search for problems or facilitate its process of
     formulating them.

     Opposed to these are the enhancing factors:

1   Members are selected in a way that utilizes their known
     abilities. (A great problem here lies in being able to identify
     the abilities that will be a potential resource.) This reinforces
     their motivation and provides a diversity of viewpoints with
     the tolerance to allow their expression.
2   The stimulation of group processes that promote the genera-
     tion of ideas; the rigorous assessment of data and ideas;
     methods of identifying the problem, of exploiting conflict,
     and of exploring alternatives.
3   Leadership acts that improve the use of information and
     encourage the flow and exchange of ideas that stimulate
     rather than arbitrate.
4   Acts that engender participation on the thesis that involve-
     ment with the decision making enhances the commitment of
     the members to what is decided.

     Steiner (1974) states that 'decision-making groups are almost
always required to perform divisible tasks'. That is, a process
comprising several separate actions in which information is
offered and discussed, background and impinging material considered, and the whole evaluated and the available alternatives
examined is set up. Because the problem that confronts a group is
seldom exactly like the last one, there are few reusable formulae

for procedure, except in the broadest sense, so a large element of improvization is necessary. Such flexibility often produces failure because the programme, recipe, or procedure eventually used is not appropriate or suitable to the problem confronted.

'Committees are primarily concerned with coming to agreements over issues where individuals or groups may disagree.'
(Argyle 1972 : 130)

Committees are formally organized talking groups designed to take decisions and solve problems. Membership varies enormously from three upwards. A committee has a formal structure of officers, chairperson, secretary, and treasurer; it is usually set up within an existing organization and is assigned its task by that organization.

Committees as groups, show marked differences to other groups. The main differences are as follows:

1 Interpersonal bonds between members are weak compared with other groups.
2 Interaction is mainly verbal.
3 Main tasks are problem solving and decision taking through verbal exchange.
4 Meetings are formal, conform to a pre-set agenda, and follow fairly elaborate and explicit rules of procedure.
5 Relationships arise as the result of the work of the group and are constituted as rapidly changing coalitions based on interest. There may be no social contact of members outside the group.

Interaction

Interaction between members is mainly verbal and governed by rules. For example, all communications have to be addressed to the chair, no member may speak for more than a specified length of time or more frequently than the rules allow, nor may any member bring up material irrelevant to the issue under discussion. A great deal of interaction takes place at the non-verbal level, e.g. eye-contact, gesture, nods, and winks, even written messages passed around among the members. The ability to use these non-verbal communications to ensure expression of one's views, to marshal aid, and to give support, is a very vital skill for the committee member.

Group development

Because of its formal structure and lack of concern about interpersonal relationships, the development of a committee is not a significant feature. Long-lasting committees with stable membership do develop expectations related to past experience, but trust is still based upon predictability. Unless some outside force threatens the committee as a whole, there is little sense of cohesion, often quite the reverse. Development in a slightly different sense does tend to occur in that a committee will produce procedures for dealing with its problems and show an increase in operational skill, however small, over its initial performance. It develops a level of expertise.

Structure

The structure is formal, though, over time, informal groupings come into existence to meet given exigencies (see sub-groups). Status within a committee is often directly related to the status of the members within the encompassing organization or to that held in other organizations represented on the committee. It is also related to the committee's perception of personality, expertise, and security of tenure of the individual member.

Sub-groups

As already noticed, committees have a flexible, informal subgroup structure of coalitions. These transient groupings are often the result of bargaining before a meeting takes place and are frequently the determining factor in the committee's decision when opposition is small due to apathy or disorganization, and the cause of conflict when competing elements have also made their bargains. Because committees are composed of people representing different interests, the formation of sub-groups and the consequent lack of overall cohesion is a salient factor of committee dynamics.

Group goals

Group goals are twofold: first to produce solutions to problems presented to the committee, and, second, to come to an agreement about what should be done. The process of problem solving requires that information about the problem and its context should be fed into the committee. This information may be first complementary, second conflicting, or third heterogeneous, but the committee's purpose is to discover as far as possible the hard facts. Remarkably enough, there is evidence to show that members are often more prepared to consider information that is not in line with their own understanding than they would as separate individuals.

The second purpose requires that the committee should examine these facts, hypothesize about them, and reach agreement.

Decision making

On each agenda item the need to reach agreement produces strong conformity pressure; the norms of behaviour are asserted at each decision point. It is here that committees show that they are prepared to take riskier decisions than individuals, probably for the following reasons:

1   Responsibility is diffused through the group.
2   Cultural norms are in favour of risk taking.
3   Some members are high risk-takers anyway.
4   The group climate favours risk taking.

Norms, standards, and values

There are the procedural norms, e.g. in voting behaviour, but there are also special rules individually created for each committee concerning timing, and what is allowed. There are norms about the general policy of the committee and about conduct and behaviour.

Cohesion

Committees are rarely cohesive because of the manner of their formation.

Influence

Conformity pressures have already been noted. However, it is necessary to point out certain influence situations not yet covered. Committees are expected by the creating organization to reach agreement about the issues submitted to them. Thus, pressures to conform come from outside as well as within the group. If the task is not being achieved, or is regarded as not being achieved by the creating organization, then members can be removed or substituted, or the whole committee abolished. Members who are representatives of other bodies are obligated to present and defend certain views and to press for other members to accept them, as they stand to gain or lose personally by the outcome.

Climate

Good leadership can induce a co-operative, hard-working climate. Differences in status, the obvious exercise of power, can inhibit it.

Environment

Environmental factors are important in that adequate access, room, and facilities are important in any group activity.

Membership

Members have varied reasons for being in the committee. They may be concerned about the task or they may have been appointed. Whatever promoted their joining, the group will affect the degree of their commitment to its success. If they have expertise and power, and are thus high-status members, the committee will spend more time discussing their ideas than those of others; they will have more influence on the final agreement whether good or bad. Good committee members need certain skills, e.g. the ability to collect, study, and assess information;

the ability to persuade, to appear emotionally uninvolved with the issues before the committee; to be concerned with what is acceptable to others; and to be able to get themselves noticed when they wish to speak.

Time

Time is an essential ingredient as many agreements are founded on the lack of it, and many decisions based on poor information because there was no time available to seek out better.

Resources

A committee's resources are twofold: first, those of its creating organization, and, second, those of, or accessible to, its members.

Size

Size is often outside the control of either the committee or its creators due to the need to cover many interests. Thus, the most effective and efficient size for the task in hand is not often available.

Open/closed nature

Most committees have the power to co-opt and are therefore open groups, a factor that tends to enhance the weak relationship structure, noted earlier, and create great reliance on the formal organization.

Activity

Committee activity is made up of mainly verbal exchange and the collection and consideration of data.

Leadership acts

The leader is the chairperson and his or her role is crucially significant in relation to the performance of the committee. The continuum of leadership style is available to the chairperson but most tend to gravitate to the directional end though with democratic overtones. The chairperson is empowered either by election or appointment to control the discussion, to influence decisions in various ways, and to try to reach conclusions that are universally acceptable. The kind of skills they need may be listed as follows:

1 Being able to recognize the problem, assess the available data, and require members to give their opinions and contributions on the central issues.
2 Concentrating on differences of opinion and trying to reach agreement.
3 Assessing the value of the available contributions and solutions in the light of any agreed policy.
4 Stimulating the committee to consider what it is proposing and to look at alternatives.
5 Ensuring that large problems are broken into manageable pieces and dealt with systematically.
6 Ensuring that the committee considers all possible solutions not just one.
7 Being custodian of the rules of procedure.

This kind of chairperson produces better results in matched groups than passive leaders can.

Contract

A contract is formed in a committee on the basis of accepting the formal procedural rules and on deciding to work for the outcomes outlined in the committee's remit.

It now remains only to look at the conditions that tend to make committees effective and those that render them ineffective.

Enhancing conditions

Committee effectiveness is enhanced when:

1 Members are able and possess different relevant skills, abilities, and resources.
2 Members are co-operative, are able to develop high commitment to the committee's aims, are able to consult freely, and feel responsible for the outcomes.
3 Members stimulate each other in the production of new, creative ideas.

4   Leadership is skilled in co-ordination, in preventing con-
    formity pressure producing inferior and premature deci-
    sions, and in producing a solution acceptable to all members.
5   The size of the committee is appropriate to the task in hand.
6   The aims of the committee are clearly understood.
7   Minorities are encouraged to participate actively.
8   Available resources are allocated to different components of
    the overall task.
9   Ideas are explored in an environment that does not produce
    immediate critical response.
10 Participation is democratic and not dominated by one or two
    powerful individuals.
11 The committee is aware that it has the power to enact the
    decisions it makes or to see that others do so.
12 Communication channels are known and kept open.
13 Sufficient time is available for discussion but not too much
    so that motivations flag.
14 Solutions can be tested and their possible effects gauged.
15 The committee knows that it is accountable for its decisions.

Retarding conditions

Apart from the normal inference that the reverse of enhancing
conditions produce retarding effects, the factors listed here seem
of major importance.

1   The decision-making procedures of the committee are im-
    posed from outside and are based on traditional practice
    rather than on what would be more useful in the given
    circumstances.
2   The members of a committee are there for a wide variety of
    reasons, often having been appointed to represent sectional
    interests so that common ground is not readily discoverable.
3   Committees are often aware of their powerlessness to imple-
    ment any decisions they make and impotency reduces
    motivation.
4   Interpersonal relationships that can cause rejection of excel-
    lent proposals on the basis of personal feeling are seldom

subject to being processed by the committee; infrequent meetings enhance this situation.

5 Not only are many committee members arbitrarily drafted, but they are also not necessarily those best equipped to deal with the issues facing their group.

Lowenstein (1971) indicated that in his opinion *size* was the constraint that produced major deficiencies in committees. It had one or two positive factors, such as increasing the resources available, but the following bad effects:

1 It decreases member participation leading to domination by a few.
2 It increases the formal nature of the interaction and the formation of sub-groups.
3 Because of 1 and 2, the committee becomes less able to use its resources. Disagreement among members increases and there is greater difficulty in following through any decisions that are made.
4 Most demands are made to meet the social and emotional needs of the members while the possibility of satisfying relationships being established decreases.
5 In general, frustration leads to dissatisfaction which, in turn, reduces members' commitment to the work of the committee.

Given these factors, it is of paramount importance that any committee should be carefully regulated as to its membership to produce maximum efficiency, while avoiding the penalties attendant upon being over large.

SUMMARY

'Suppose that you and I are members of a six-member committee to raise funds for underprivileged children. Suppose that you are intelligent, creative, athletic, wealthy and personable. I'm feeling competitive with you. Because of these feelings if you propose an idea for raising funds, I will be prone to find fault with it, to ridicule it, to argue it down, even if it's a good idea – *especially* if it's a good idea.' (Aronson 1976 : 299)

Aronson's statement demonstrates the havoc to committee efficiency that unexposed member rivalries can wreak. He also believes that the decisions arrived at by committees are limited by cognitive dissonance so that in the early stages of decision making members will reject information that is not consonant with the data, convictions, and beliefs that they already hold. On balance, Aronson sees group decision making as of limited efficiency. Given that limited efficiency exists, why do organizations continue to set up committees? I think the answer must lie in the fact that they deliver a major part of the expected goods.

Committees are time-limited groups and so need expert co-ordination to avoid wasting time on unproductive manoeuvres. That means a directive, controlling leadership pattern is exploited. They contain members with diffuse aims, often enough irreconcilable, so an imposed structure is necessary that creates artificial but agreed boundaries within which even conflicting interest groups can work if not together exactly, at least not in open confrontation. This kind of ritual structure of necessity inhibits the open expression of personal antagonisms and pays the cost of hidden agendas and probable sabotage. Committees have clearly defined functions, shared responsibilities, and access to more human resources than any individual. They can, and do, exert pressure on their members and, because personal factors are seldom at stake, they can produce answers.

For all these reasons (and others stated earlier), committees seem to develop the group processes and constraints that facilitate a particular kind of limited group operation. It is not dependent upon the time and contact, the shared experience necessary to develop an awareness in each member of belonging to a caring, trusting, and supportive unit. It uses just the processes that enable it to function in the absence of such factors by creating an agreed and accepted system.

Committees, then, can deal with information, in fact with huge complexities of information, but they cannot deal with emotional problems very well because their own emotional stability is not, and cannot be, built into their formal procedural structure.

Problems in committee functioning may be reduced if the personal characteristics of members, their ability, and their prior experience do not develop a unanimity that precludes any discussion, nor even a powerful clique to enforce a majority role. The influence of bias can be avoided by a reasonable selection procedure, by keeping the size of the committee smaller rather than larger, and by creating a clear and unequivocal formal structure to reduce the effect of personal characteristics. Efficiency may also be improved by the production of an organization that is able to search for problems and that develops a technique of scanning more possibilities than usual by not focusing too early.

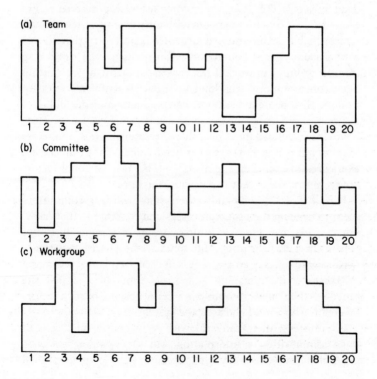

(a) Team

1 2 3 4 5 6 7 8 9 10 11 12 13 14 15 16 17 18 19 20

(b) Committee

1 2 3 4 5 6 7 8 9 10 11 12 13 14 15 16 17 18 19 20

(c) Workgroup

1 2 3 4 5 6 7 8 9 10 11 12 13 14 15 16 17 18 19 20

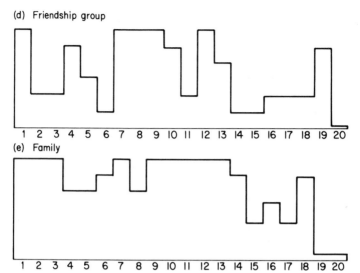

Figure 4 A comparison of the profiles of intensity of involvement of the factors affecting group outcome in five 'natural' groupings.

The height of the column shows a rough estimate of the intensity of use of that 'factor-affecting' in that particular group.[4]

Key

'Factors-affecting'

1	Interaction	11	Environment
2	Group development	12	Membership
3	Social structure	13	Time
4	Sub-group formation	14	Resources
5	Group goals	15	Size
6	Decision-making process	16	Open/closed state
7	Norms, standards, and values	17	Activity
8	Cohesion	18	Leadership acts
9	Group influence	19	Selection
10	Group climate	20	Contract

[4] As this book is concerned with the elements of design of groups used for specific purposes, these profiles, which show roughly the levels of the 'factors-affecting' outcome that appear to generate efficiency in each of five 'natural' groups, are a visible reminder of design difference. The components are the same but they are combined in different quantities producing a unique custom-built model in each case. That such design difference comes about in groups with long histories of use should serve to indicate that the general features built into each model equate with successful functioning.

Committee performance can be enhanced by positive utiliz-ation of resources in terms of ability, of motivation, and the diversity of experience related to the freedom to generate ideas, to examine facts and material rigorously, and to exploit conflict. Most of this kind of activity comes under the rubric of skilled leadership, which should create an improved flow of information and encourage a better use of it.

A committee functioning effectively has most of the factors just discussed operating positively and, in such a situation, demonstrates as clearly as possible the element of design that allows such a performance.

It remains to be seen in the next section whether groups created to meet equally specific circumstances but without, in most cases, such a long history of adaptation and modification, show such clear design differences.

PART THREE

The Probable Effects of Group Processes in the Design and Function of Special Environments

INTRODUCTION

'What treatment by whom is most effective for this individual with that specific problem and under which set of circumstances?' (Paul in Smith 1980 : 20)

It has always appeared to be accepted that when the 'normal' processes of living in a society do not produce a desirable end result, some form of environment can be specially designed or created to deal with such situations. At the simple end of the continuum these special environments exercise a containment function. They hold selected people in a manner that more or less separates them from the general society, thereby reducing the effect of their presence, whatever that has been.

Special environments can also be designed to offer punishment, treatment, care, training, and security – in short, to supply needs that people are not able to supply for themselves, or needs that are defined as such by society (the need for care or control, for example). The essential point about this is that it is not necessarily natural environments, in the sense of environments already in existence, that are used in these circumstances, but environments that are specifically designed to produce predictable effects. Good examples of natural environments are used as, for instance, when a child is placed with a foster family when his or her family of origin has provided inadequate caring or socializing. But this form of use of an existing environment is strictly limited for two obvious reasons. First, there is clearly a limit to which new units can be integrated into an existing group without the nature of that group, which made it acceptable in the first place, being changed. Second, the number of such 'good' natural environments must fall far short of the need for them.

Another consideration that may be overlooked is that the kind of environment that could be required to meet a given set of circumstances does not occur in a natural state at all, i.e. the normal processes of human intercourse have not generated such an amalgam.

The basic implication of this is that the modification of behaviours low on social acceptability can be achieved in environments specifically created of factors known to encourage the development of change in the target behaviours. In a word, an environment for change can be designed. Now, design implies that the effects of given elements both singly and in combination, can be predicted, and herein lies the problem. In many areas the nature of the cause-effect relationship of environmental factors and behavioural patterns is neither clear nor precise. The rules of design must therefore be equally crude. However, once again the available knowledge exceeds the use of it and many designed environments fail to benefit from the recorded experience of previous experiments.

What is clear, however, is the fact that not all social scientists accept the primacy of environmental factors in changing or even in affecting behaviour. Newman states that,

'If one wishes to know about the impact that an organisation such as a school or a business has upon an individual, an examination of a diagram or map of the organisational structure or the physical settings will be of only limited use. The investigator must go into the settings and measure the quantity and quality of interaction that the people in the setting are having with one another. He must learn which messages come through most clearly and most often, who sends messages, how the people who receive the messages react to them and how the variety of settings in the environment serve as a network of interactive market places where messages are traded.'   (Newman 1976 : 44)

The argument here is that environmental influence on behaviour is indirect, acting through its effect upon facilitating or diminishing interaction and communication. So be it, the need for an increased understanding of the cause-and-effect connection be-tween facilitating and diminishing environments and the level of interaction and communication can still provide us with the basis of design that can make maximum use of these connections.

In this section we shall be looking at group-containing organ-izations that have been specially created, looking, for example, at the way residential institutions have been set up, how thera-peutic environments and communities have been created, and at groups that have been brought into being to deal with specific problems. Our main purpose will be to see whether, or to what extent, the lessons about the components of effective group design have been applied. Here are three areas where design factors have to be important and in fact are often claimed to be just that. The evidence tends to show that whatever design features have been considered, many others have been ignored or not considered sufficiently. Basically, the fault, if fault it is, lies with inadequate information. It is simple enough to enumerate the omissions, but it is often very difficult to point to sources of information that could lead to a more considered approach.

9

RESIDENTIAL INSTITUTIONS

INTRODUCTION

'It is difficult to estimate how many people sit down each day to an institutional breakfast. More accurate guesses can be made of the size of some groups than others. Children in residential care provided by Local Authorities or in hospitals and boarding schools number about 220,000 but how many elderly are sheltered in residential homes, many of which are private, is much more difficult to estimate.'   (Millham *et al.* 1980 : 1)

There is a large range of residential institutions in our society, but they all have several things in common. They are all concerned with bringing collections of individuals together to live in close proximity, they all constrain their members, most accommodate a large number of everyday life functions, and, by the norms of our society, most are artificial creations.

It is quite obvious that if large numbers of people have to be treated, confined, taught, separated from others, and looked after, then the dictates of the economic use of resources insist that these functions should be done in one institution. But this does not explain very well why a condition of residence in an institution is so important, except when a crucial part of the institution's purpose has to do with containment or security. Certain conditions, such as ill-health and the impracticality of being moved, dictate the residential state, but where similar functions are performed in non-residential institutions, what is the reason for using a living-in condition?

Often enough residential institutions are described as constituting a 'group living' condition. By this is meant that people who under normal circumstances would live completely separate lives are brought together for some reason to live under one roof. One interesting fact that emerges from this is that where some form of socialization or re-socialization is the principal aim of the residential establishment, then the basic group influence process of conformity is highly desirable and the institution is nearly always designed to ensure maximum conformity from its residents. Yet those residential institutions whose major function is caring also generate a system in which conformity is also a large element because it produces economy of management. So, although established for very different reasons, the systems of these institutions bear a marked resemblance to each other and often produce similar effects in their residents though in different degree. In one case, therefore, the conformity factor is heavily designed-in because it is believed that this will help to bring about the desired re-socialization, whereas in the other conformity has nothing whatever to recommend it in terms of the resident's needs; it is related to administrative convenience and economy. In the latter case, the level of conformity pressure could be reduced with evident gain to the resident. All residential establishments therefore have many things in common, though used for different purposes. Many of the common factors are almost incidental to the express purpose of the institution, some are wasteful, and some are actually counterproductive.

Therapeutic environments, as we shall see later, contain a larger design element in their construction and organization. Their express purpose is to use elements of the general residential situation that are known to enhance the achievement of the institution's aims, and to design-out, or reduce, the effect of elements that are useless or deleterious to the aims.

What will tend to emerge from our discussion of residential institutions is that many functions in the residential situation mitigate against the purposes for which they are used with a consequent low success rate. Equally, it is true that if influencing processes were more clearly understood, and used to modify both the use and design of residential institutions, they could be fundamentally changed for the better.

Residential institutions in general fulfil some of the functions listed below. They:

1 Isolate, segregate, insulate, contain, and restrict access to others.

2 Define boundaries, set rules, control activities, structure time, and routinize.

3 Define the population in which contacts are made.

4 Define status and roles of that population, and create forms of speech and modes of address that are appropriate to them.

5 Provide security and freedom from the need to be self-governing in many aspects of life by creating a new social order.

6 Provide a given standard of existence and care.

7 Reduce or eliminate self-esteem, choice, and decision making.

8 Offer the possibility of change, growth, support, learning, treatment, training, guidance, or behaviour modification.

9 Offer the opportunity to fulfil a particular form, function, or a style of life not possible in the larger society.

10 Create a pool of resources that can be shared.

11 Operate as agents of society in the matter of punishment.

12 Provide a transient or permanent home, sustenance, or entertainment.

13 Provide a place of meeting, of exposure to change agents.

14 Provide a reference group for residents and ex-residents.

15 Provide a milieu for residential workers.

Though long and complex, this list by no means covers the total functions of residential institutions, but it is reasonable to assume that some of these functions being simpler than others are more readily attainable. We must now look at what residential institutions are, including examples of the main classes of institution, and then we must attempt to see them as complex organizations composed of many different groupings. Taking this latter viewpoint will allow us to use the group-process analysis of the various forms of residential institution and eventually to draw some conclusions about the efficient design use of the 'factors-affecting'.

WHAT ARE RESIDENTIAL INSTITUTIONS?

'Compliance is universal, existing in all social units. It is a major element of the relationship between those who have power and those over whom they exercise it.'

(Etzioni 1980 : 87)

In a general sense, a residential institution is one in which selected people are taken to live in a particular residence because it is believed that what are seen as their needs, or society's requirements of them, can best be met in this kind of situation. This belief is supported by many factors of very diverse natures, e.g. similarity of situation and the economy of numbers. It is economically cheaper to deal with several people who require residential facilities or the kind of looking-after that a residential setting can offer and whose requirements stem from the same or similar causes, gathered together in one institution. This is often put forward as being based upon the grounds of efficiency, but, fundamentally, economy of effort and provision are probably more important.

Gathering people together in a residential establishment generates a clearly defined demarcation analagous to the 'in' or 'out' states of groups *vis-à-vis* other groups, and of group members *vis-à-vis* non-group people. As we shall see, this physical boundary is often taken as delineating a 'group' and, in the sense that the residents occupy contiguous space, are aware of each other's presence, interact and exert influence, and abide (to some degree or other) within the norms of the establishment, this is true. However, it is equally true that large institutions contain many groups within the population of residents, where the factors in common are greater in number than for the population as a whole, and where the operation of group processes comprises a larger and more significant part of the situational dynamic.

All residential institutions are 'people-processing' organizations. That is, they are organizations set up to 'process' people. People are the raw material of the organization and its end product. The institution is a place in which the raw material can be contained to be worked upon by the staff who operate the organization. This must lead us directly to the point Etzioni was making in the quotation at the head of this section. Residential institutions are also complex organizations with a clear power structure that involves an element of compliance.

Blau and Scott (1962) classified formal organizations on the basis of 'prime beneficiary', i.e. who benefits? Residential institutions fall squarely into the third category of their four-part classification: 'Service organizations – where the client group is the prime beneficiary', but they also spill over into category four where the beneficiary is the public at large. So, a residential institution may be defined as a complex social organization in which the members of the organization are resident and in which there is a clear demarcation of professional staff possessing and using power, and residents who possess little power and whose response to the system is one of compliance.

Now it could be argued that in essence this structure bears a marked resemblance to a group that has a directive leader legitimized in his or her role by some larger, accepted, and recognized power – only the scale is larger. This is true, and to a large extent the problems that apply to such a group in terms of status difference, dependence, and comparative neglect of the use of the group itself and its resources, apply with added force in residential institutions. But there is another problem: whereas the directive group leader is a unit of power, the unit of power in an organization is not one person but many, a corporate unit with diverse natures, beliefs, attitudes, skills, and intelligence, the attributes of the component members of that unit. Such a unit cannot offer security or continuity of performance in the same way that a single autonomous leader can. The element of unpredictability has been increased many times. The individual is solely responsible, he or she can review their performance, monitor its effects, and be aware of how they are responding to their involvement. The mechanisms exist in his or her own personal and professional skills. Such mechanisms in corporate directive units have to be first recognized as being needed and, second, created.

Obviously, residential institutions are places where people live. Often they are not places where they would have chosen to live; that choice has been taken from them by elements in their circumstances that have led others to decide that such a condition of residence should be offered or required in their own best interests. The ensuing separation from others of their 'natural' milieu may be punitive in intent, necessary on the grounds of hazard or security, or necessary merely on the basis that there is nothing else that can cope with a given situation, e.g. homelessness. But such enforced residency brings about a situation that is often referred to as 'group-living', and because this brings into closer focus the group-containing nature of all complex organizations, we must look at group-living in more detail.

Maier said about group living that it 'refers to the everyday experience each individual faces while he shares the routine of daily life within a group, namely, awakening, waiting, eating, division of labor and above all, reflection upon outward life experiences' (1961 : 125). When we looked briefly at the family earlier, it was obvious that this group is the 'natural' living group in the sense that it is the group wherein we all get our first experience of sharing our daily routines with other people. It is the training ground for any subsequent group-living situations we may enter, as it is for all other group situations. But the unique feature of the family, e.g. its bonds, do not occur in other group-living situations in the same way, and so the whole structure has a compellingly different affectionate base.

In essence this means that the satisfaction of some needs in group-living can never be met; some can be met in a different way from the family group response, and others can be met in the same way. Depending on how well major needs are met by the family group, group-living can range all the way from being eminently satisfying to being totally unrewarding. Some prisoners and mental hospital patients find more satisfaction in being incarcerated in their respective institutions than in being free and self-supporting. We tend to argue that their social competence is of a low order either by reason of socialized incompetence or by accident, which destroys an operative level of social competence.

Thus, group-living is often regarded as an 'artificial' state and most are prepared to tolerate it only on the understanding that it will be a transient experience. But by its very nature, existence in the 'presence-of-others', it must offer the possibility of much shared experience, of being compelled to acknowledge the rights of others, their needs, one's dependence, of increased interaction, of intimacy, and of the recognition of common plight. In other words, group-living offers (the offers are not necessarily taken up), most of the factors needed to generate a cohesive group. Role models abound, familiarity generates some degree of predictability and thus of security and perhaps trust, all factors that in true group situations can lead to learning and personal growth.

However, often enough these shared experiences are mainly with one sub-group of the system and much less with the other. As we shall see later, identification tends to follow the distinction between staff and residents, what has been referred to as the 'managers' and the 'managed', the 'processors' and the 'processed'.

Jones (1967) indicated that residential institutions 'exist for a specific purpose or group of purposes, e.g. to heal, to shelter, to confine, to teach, to protect'.

It must be obvious that these generalizations could be expanded indefinitely and that there are many possible classifications of residential institutions. This could hardly be otherwise given the enormous range of activities encompassed by such organizations. For our purpose it will suffice to look briefly at three classifications. These are residential institutions that are primarily custodial, or therapeutic, or punitive.

Custodial

Custodial is used here in the sense of 'guardianship' or 'care' rather than in its more common usage of imprisonment. The kind of institutions considered in this large classification are all those that offer a residential situation of care. This can apply to clients ranging from small children, through the homeless, and those with transient needs, to the aged and infirm. In fact, the element of custody is perhaps basic to all residential institutions even if their prime function or aim lies within the sphere of one of the other major groupings.

A great problem arises here in the nature of the client groups admitted to residential institutions. For instance, the degree of ability to be self-governing varies enormously – the degree to which society wants residents to be self-governing also varies enormously. Many who are capable, i.e. socially competent, are exactly the people that society requires to be held institutionally where their capabilities cannot be exercised to their own gain and the detriment of some part of society.

However, for most people who are in 'custodial' residential establishments, the main function of the institution is to supply a living base, a replacement for the natural home environment, which has either been lost, or is no longer appropriate, or which for other reasons is considered unsuitable. Now 'care' in this sense can range from the simple provision of accommodation – a place to sleep, physical care, and food – to the other extreme of a special regime designed to meet urgent physical and psychological needs. In any case, the institution is a complex organization that seems to hold its clients within itself; their presence is essential to the existence of the organization but the element of influence they have is negligible. Dynamically, such residents tend to remain committed to their individual interests. Few of the pressures that would compel them to unite and find common cause are available and so the system is often described as a service directed to the client, that is, to the individual not to the statistical group known as clients. This service orientation marks another major distinguishing factor in the organization and has generated the concept that residential custodial situations are 'people-processing' systems; the 'processors', who are professional and assume that they know what they are doing, and the 'processed', who are the raw material, as it were, of the system and often very ignorant of what it is all about, apart from appreciating the major effects it may have had upon their quality of life.

Custodial in the sense of 'containing' or 'holding' constitutes a fairly large element of what residential institutions provide and, as we shall see later, this containing function, while increasing the difference between the processors and the processed, does so in ways that bring into play sufficient pressure to create a much more cohesively functioning sub-group from the 'processed' than the guardianship function can do. The difference is the unity of the treatment accorded to the 'contained' in any one institution. Almost alone this factor renders individuals normally concerned with their own self-interest aware that survival is no longer easily possible as a discrete unit. Survival depends upon conformity to the immediate containing structure.

Institutions that have a primarily containing function are not, therefore, exclusively directed to the welfare of their clients, which would involve a considerable shift of attitude on the part of the staff and a consequent loss of individual security. It is no longer possible for the client of such an institution to convince him- or herself that however much the system irks or worries, it will ultimately increase the level of satisfaction because that was what it was designed to achieve. For instance, the personal indignities of hospital eventually produce a better functioning person, the personal affronts of a containing institution do not have such a curative or ameliorative end in view but are part of an often humiliating restraint. Personal safety can only be assured by banding together at the cost of the loss of some individual freedom of action but for the reward of being able to survive the system.

Therapeutic

'Through socialisation into group living, the individual comes in effect to make assumptions about himself. Although these assumptions are about himself, they nonetheless are delineated in terms of his approved relationships to other members of the group and in terms of the collective enterprise – his rightful contribution to it and his rightful share in it.'

(Goffman 1969b : 183)

As therapeutic communities and environments will be dealt with in some detail in the next chapter, only a brief statement is in order here. The major factors of residential institutions with a therapeutic aim are first, convenience and, second, isolation.

Convenience In this case, convenience means that all the elements constitute the therapeutic endeavour – the patient, the professionals, the resources, and accessibility are all found together in one place. Whatever the therapy may be, from straight residential care of a purely maintenance kind, through the whole range of physical dysfunction, to the care of those who are mentally disturbed, this factor is primary. It makes the difference between being able to deal with the presenting problems adequately with minimum loss of efficiency and a kind of ad hoc approach, or at least a piecemeal approach, which is time-consuming as well as being inefficient. Of course, the 'convenience' is attached much more to the professional end of the therapeutic endeavour and, as we shall see later, the design of such endeavours has frequently been considered only from the point of view of the process and not from that of the people to whom the process has been applied.

In terms of group dynamics, this has resulted in the processed being clearly unable to influence the outcome very much except by the drastic process of opting out of it. Members of an organization who perceive that although the organization is going to impinge on their lives to a great extent and yet have no chance to influence the process, perceive their helpless and powerless state. Where opting out is not physically feasible, dependence and apathy are common responses to this perception in all kinds of groups. As Goffman (1969) points out, the client's rightful share in and contribution to the organization tend to be diminished as are his or her perceptions about him- or herself.

So 'convenience' often means that the environment, resources, and so on are designed to facilitate the professionally desired outcome. If this outcome coincides with providing the client with a high level of satisfaction and, more importantly, whether this fact is clearly understood as such by the individual being processed in his or her own terms, then the chances are that the balance of satisfaction will be tilted in favour of the individual accepting the situation on the basis of deferred gratification. Sadly, the understanding that would make current costs acceptable is not easily come by. It is either withheld as a matter of professional judgement or couched in terms completely or largely incomprehensible due to the lack of suitable reference points, or general understanding is lacking anyway.

Isolation   The concept of convenience cannot really be looked at separately. It has to be regarded in conjunction with the concept of 'isolation'. Residential situations are almost always made available because the natural living conditions of the individual have proved to be inadequate in one or more major facets. Thus, children are committed to care because of gross and possibly damaging inadequacies in their natural family situation, people are committed to prison because their natural living conditions are inadequate to protect society from their depradations and very inadequate for the administration of any punishment, and so on. The very existence of a residential institution means that those who live in it are totally or partially excluded from living elsewhere. They are isolated from the other larger community; they are contained.

As far as therapeutic endeavours are concerned, this isolation tends to mean that (a) the residents are readily available and can be monitored, or that (b) they are separated from harmful influences that may have been the cause of their problems in the first instance, be they psychological or physical, and that (c) the isolating process will enhance the therapeutic process by reducing other influences thus creating an intensity of experience that has frequently to be used in lieu of long periods of time that are not often available. What tends to happen is that exposure to a system, which is possible in a residential situation, has a swamping effect, generating norms of behaviour relevant to the therapeutic process and, depending on the degree of exclusion of other influences, providing almost the only reality.

It is a characteristic of exclusive groups that they mediate reality for their members. Often this generates a great sense of security but such cohesion can also cause stagnation, a loss of contact with the larger society, and a loss of any desire to return to that society. This causes great problems when return is the essential end or product of the therapeutic endeavour.

'the new cohesive, social groups will provide the individual with a greater sense of belonging and purpose than is afforded by mechanistic society. However, the group dynamic literature is fraught with examples of how cohesion in groups can lead to shared distortions and unproductive conforming behaviour.' (Miller 1976 : 234)

Punitive

'We very generally find staff employing what are called admission procedures, such as taking a life history, photographing, weighing, fingerprinting, assigning numbers, searching, listing personal possessions for storage, undressing, bathing, disinfecting, haircutting, issuing institutional clothing, instructing as to rules and assigning to quarters . . . the new arrival allows himself to be shaped and coded into an object that can be fed into the administrative machinery of the establishment, to be worked on smoothly by routine operations.' (Goffman 1968 : 92)

The process described above was called 'trimming' by Goffman. By this he meant that entry into a 'total institution' was a ritual of segregation, of loss of identity and status, the first step of being fitted into a new social order where the major purpose is segregation/isolation and the secondary aims may be concerned with change.

The argument about whether punitive institutions should be humane actually turns logically not so much on the priority of punishment over change as on what actually constitutes punishment. If punishment is regarded as loss of freedom of choice in some considerable areas of life style (e.g. no choice about what one does for most of the time, nor with whom it is done, or when, or where, or for how long), then logically the residential institution should not also add the indignity of a poor quality of care or poor physical standards. But if punishment is regarded as requiring a diminution of *all* aspects of a person's life and not just in the elements of choice, then prisons, for instance, should logically be the places of human degradation that they have often become in wartime with death as the final deterrent.

But for many who go to places of correction, the regime that is meant to be punishing is actually rewarding in the sense that it provides a more reasonable standard of living than can be obtained outside. Also, in many cases whatever else it may be, detention, even for longish periods, is seen as a cost that is accepted because the ultimate rewards of criminality are of a high enough order to maintain the balance well into the credit side.

When these factors are considered in conjunction with the dynamics that pressurize the residents of punitive institutions, by making inevitable the recognition of overriding similarities with their peers and of essential differences from the professional staff, then the function of punishment in such institutions must be considerably reduced. This is a major point, because, as we have seen, residential institutions that do not give one major sub-group, i.e. the residents, sufficient cause to sink their differences in dealing with a survival situation and form a reasonably cohesive and conforming alternative culture, stand some chance of successful work with individuals and jointly – the two major sub-groups working for a common end.

It is significant that treatment units that initially employ an extremely punitive approach with clients, such as addicts, make it clear that apart from testing the viability of the motivation to benefit from treatment, such degradation and destruction of esteem is the bottom or initiation phase of becoming a member of that particular mini-society. The cost is well balanced by an achievable reward. Prisons, borstals, and detention centres have a large 'cost' and a very small reward item in their programmes for the clients. It is not surprising, therefore, that the rewards necessary to balance the inflicted costs have to be sought in some other way. The transmitted culture of the client sub-group usually offers these rewards in terms of friendship, support, and, above all, information on how to survive.

To return to the opening point of this section briefly, if punishment is defined as a definite reduction in the freedom to make choices affecting everyday concerns, then residential institutions of punishment make this objective easy to obtain because environment and behaviour can be controlled. But we know that the effect of any situation on any individual is very largely brought about by his or her perception of it, and many who enter punitive establishments have attitudes to those establishments that are at some considerable variance with those of the designers and recommenders. So, although the primary task of isolation from the larger community obviously occurs, such isolation, although protective for its duration, does not necessarily constitute the element or degree of punishment that society might have desired.

OPERATING CONSTRAINTS

'It may be that where an institution has reasonably good material standards, where it is run with a reasonable sensitivity to the needs of human rights of its residents; where it is small, or where sub-groups can be organised on a meaningful basis; above all where the institution has a useful purpose, and offers better facilities than any of the actual alternatives, the fact that it involves a pattern of living other than that of the nuclear family may not in itself be harmful.' (Jones 1967 : 15)

Jones was suggesting that much of the criticism directed at residential institutions was provoked by bad institutions and not by institutions in general. But my point must be that even good institutions do not pay sufficient attention to the 'design' function of the group processes. Let us analyse briefly what we have discovered about residential institutions in the light of the 'factors-affecting' as we did in the previous section concentrating on the factors that seem salient.

All the major group constraints are or paramount importance.

Environment

In what Jones calls 'the literature of dysfunction', the nature of the buildings, the atmosphere, the routine, the whole milieu in which the residents and staff operate are quoted over and over again as one of the most important elements in generating the life style of residents; e.g. Goffman's concept of 'batch-living', Barton's idea of 'institutional neurosis', and the Morrisses' use of the word 'prisonisation'. These general ideas about the effect of institutions on their inhabitants are so numerous and so similar that they must be referring to a clearly observable environmental effect.

Of course, the environment is not solely responsible. But all the other factors, such as structure, norms, standards, values, climate, and influence, which all contribute to its overall nature and maintain it in existence, are equally to blame.

Membership

Any institution is comprised of people, but the qualities of the members of a residential institution are of cardinal importance in that at least some of those qualities and characteristics will be the prime reason for the institution's existence. Perhaps the interesting feature of this particular constraint is that the qualities of members are not only assumed, with certain notable exceptions, but also the nature of the institutions that meet those qualities and needs are assumed. Consider the fact that institutions have a function. This is related to particular assessed needs so people who do not have those needs should not be readmitted to that institution. The population of any institution is therefore made up of people in a like state of need. The characteristics that made the individual a client are enormously and disproportionately represented in the institutional population. What effect does such gross imbalance have on the qualities of membership? Very few answers have been realistically offered to this question except straight affirmation that an effect must be there, and that it is neither a positive nor a beneficial one.

Old people are expected to behave like old people – unanimity of behaviour leads to administrative convenience; conformity with expectations becomes a big issue that results in the many accusations of institutionalization. What residents in an institution can do is seldom clear.

'There are admitted dangers in treating inmates as though they were incapable of independent action, and equal dangers in assuming total social functioning where it does not exist.'

(Jones 1967 : 13–14)

Time

The factor of time has many facets as far as residential institutions are concerned. But let us just take one, the duration of stay. This ranges from a few hours to a lifetime and must affect not only the resident's attitude to the institution but the attitude of the institution to the resident. Clearly the duration of residence affects what the institution might attempt in terms of care, treatment, punishment, learning, or rehabilitation. Group dynamics would indicate that these attitudes are related not just to the overall factor of duration of stay, but also to different stages within the stay. Group members behave in significantly different ways at the beginning, in the middle, and at the end of a group's life, as witness the voluminous literature on the development process in groups. Also, what is tolerable when an end is known and can be worked towards may become intolerable when no definite time of cessation is available.

Structure

The structure of residential institutions, in fact the subgroup formation within the organization, often appears to be a possible cause of inefficiency. Goffman (1968) describes very clearly the power structure of the managing sub-group where techniques for the reduction of the residents' self-esteem are thorough and effective. There is little doubt that this form of exercise of power also serves to generate a cohesive, supportive, and protective unity among the 'managed'. It provides an almost impenetrable barrier to any change approaches that may also be part of the basic structure. For example, exercise of power leads to reduction of self-esteem that in turn leads to distrust and defensive submission. Change is dependent upon the enhancement of trust not its diminution.

Where institutions have attempted to reduce this dissonance by diminishing the difference between the managers and the managed, the supra-structure has usually intervened at some stage to highlight the artificiality of such an environment, at least in our current society. This is not to say that reduction of difference is a fallacy (it is not), but often the amount of the reduction and its total coverage are so much at odds with the observable and practised power structure (e.g. who decides that the reduction of difference shall be undertaken?) that what could have been acceptable and effective in smaller doses can only be accepted by a suspension of disbelief. This is not a good basis on which to found enduring change.

The discussion of the 'factors-affecting' is endless. But two final points need to be made. First, not all residential institutions have members who have been drafted there. Some have residents who not only have voluntarily become members but who see membership as an eminently desirable end. The balance of satisfaction is immediately in a different state, as far as they are concerned, and the level to which conformity can be expected and produced is on a much higher scale. Because the possession of such a high level of satisfaction exists, the many other satisfaction-reducing elements will have to be enormous before alternatives become either attractive or taken.

Second, cost. The efficient use of residential situations must be an expensive programme involving reductions in the size of some institutions, increased staffing, and hugely increased resources of skill and knowledge. Often enough the factor of cost is the one constraint that dictates what is possible even though its effect may be diminished by extra inputs such as energy, enthusiasm, and time. These factors are also inevitably costly if not in direct cash terms. The dead hand of costs is quite obliterating but some leeway for change exists in the fact that the available resources are not necessarily being distributed in the most effective way.

The lessons are clear, I think, that the information exists, though in a relatively crude state, that would enable whatever resources there are to be used more efficiently for the residents' benefit.

'In our view, the first step towards meeting the needs of these children is to provide a planned environment. Such an environment provides not only a supportive framework for a variety of treatments, but also an environment which is in itself therapeutic and, as such, it may be all that is needed for many children for whom no special form of treatment has been prescribed.'   (Advisory Council on Child Care 1970 : 8)

10

THERAPEUTIC ENVIRONMENTS
AND COMMUNITIES

INTRODUCTION

'I began to realise that the therapeutic community as I had
known it was an early model of an open system, before
Systems Theory was a recognised entity. I have become
increasingly convinced that the social organisation of a hospital, or a church, or a classroom (Jones 1974) will influence the
behaviour of the subjects in ways as yet not well understood.'

(Jones 1979 : 3)

The ultimate point about what I have called the 'constraints' is
that they affect the process and eventual outcome of any group
that operates within their sphere of influence. Paramount among
the constraints is the environment, which, taken in the very
broadest sense, could include everything that surrounds the
group, everything of which it is composed. But even if other
constraints are acknowledged to exist and environmental factors
limited to those listed in Chapter 2, the strength of environmental influence on group outcomes is still enormous.

It is little wonder that this influence should be taken into
account when planning environments to meet given specific
situations. The recognition of design factors relating to an
environment has been known for centuries. Religions have
created impressive buildings to generate awe of the gods wor-
shipped inside; governments and rulers have erected palaces to
generate a sense of wealth and power; and prisons have created a

powerful sense of fear, isolation, and punishment. People have constantly been struck by the emotional responses produced by natural environments of very different qualities.

One of the problems, as yet unsolved, in the creation of environments that generate specific responses, is how far the response is triggered by the environment and how much it springs from the expectations and previous experience of those who enter it. In a sense the answer is irrelevant. If an environment is to be created to generate a particular response, it is necessary only to know the kind of expectations any given society is likely to have of the kind of environment one anticipates producing. Thus, what is an awe-inspiring situation to one group who have traditional expectations that such a situation should be responded to with awe, will have a quite different effect on a group without this preconditioning.

A large part of any environment consists of the people it contains and the behaviour patterns they exhibit. Rules of conduct and behaviour patterns in general are perhaps the easiest of the environmental variables to manipulate. So, history records many attempts to establish communities where behaviour is regulated on the basis of different norms from those of the larger society that contains the community. Often enough such communities, aware of the contaminating effect that the norms of the larger society can have, attempt to isolate themselves from it, not only psychologically but also physically. Sanctions may well be exercised against members who transgress the rules of segregation.

Contamination is especially likely when the habits of the old life are strong and compelling, and can give continuing support to their existence in the individual. In this situation the influence of environment is powerfully obvious and stringent separation from its effects has to be maintained until another set of habits is rooted firmly enough to withstand exposure.

How effective can designed environments be? I suspect that a definitive answer cannot be given though evidence points to the possibility that the answer should be 'very great'. Ethical considerations, considerations of what might happen to the people involved, surround the experimental pursuit of the answer. So, as in most important areas of the understanding of social behaviour, only partial verification of ideas is possible or ethically desirable.

Whatever kinds of therapeutic community and environment are created, two major problems and a host of minor ones seem to arise. First, there is the problem of artificiality, of creating a situation that is abnormal and cannot be sustained. Out of this comes the second major problem, which is concerned with transfer back to the original living community and the loss of support it entails for any newly acquired behaviour patterns. The second problem in some religious communities is answered by not returning to the host community. For many therapeutic communities this is not a feasible proposition unless continuing physical or mental care is necessary.

WHAT ARE THEY?

'The four fundamental themes originally suggested by Rapoport (1960) as characterising the therapeutic community are still worthy of general acceptance. They are: Democratization, Permissiveness, Reality-Confrontation and Communalism.'

(Morrice 1979 : 49)

Therapeutic communities appear to be based on the assumption that change, in behavioural terms, has to come from within the individual. That is, each individual has to become convinced of his or her need to change, to become aware that such change is possible, and ultimately that he or she must bring it about. Essentially this thesis is a rejection of the medical model and of any other form of paternalism. Hence, it eschews external direction, obedience from respect of expertise and the charismatic individual, and any dependence apart from group- or self-dependence.

In a society in which everyone is brought up to recognize specialization as something eminently desirable, such a move requires some explanation. Of all the things that human beings deal with, it is arguable that one knows least about oneself. In particular, the individual knows little about his or her most important asset, his or her 'mind', the processes of thinking and feeling and how they operate to allow each of us to live in a world that appears to possess some order. Even more particularly he or she knows even less about what goes wrong with these processes, if that is what it is, and thus is somewhat handicapped in doing much to ameliorate or end such situations. However little the individual knows about him- or herself, what they know, they know directly from within; what others can know of the individual can only be known from outside by comparing observable behaviour against the available collected data of human behaviour. Thus, if it is the case that we develop in such a way that each lives in a separate world, as Kelly (1970) says, then it could be logical to argue that the only person who really knows anything directly about the problems of the individual's mental functioning is the individual involved although he or she may not have the ability or desire to communicate that understanding to anyone else. It is then also reasonable to argue that this self same individual, being the only one possessed of real understanding, is the only one able to do anything about it, even though he or she may need considerable help and guidance in the process.

This argument inevitably leads one stage further. After the individual, those best equipped to understand him or her are those in a similar situation. Thus, the expert is one whose knowledge is derived from the observation of others and the collection and structuring of data into generalization. The individual sufferer or experiencer, on the other hand, has first-hand experience and knows more or less precisely what is involved in his or her own case. It is assumed that this level of personal experience and how it has been coped with must be nearer in kind and in quality to the experience of another individual similarly afflicted than the generalized ideas of the non-afflicted expert.

Of course this is not entirely true, and for this reason designers of therapeutic environments often combine both elements to take advantage of both aspects. This means that the problem of status has to be dealt with and it is often done in such a manner that the people in the community have to make some massive adjustments to suspend their disbelief. But theoretically the idea of the 'expert' and the individual combining their resources in a climate of equality is essentially very logical. Add to this the third element, the credibility of peers, the similarity of their experience, and the opportunity to learn how others have coped, and a fairly potent therapeutic mixture has apparently been arrived at.

However, therapeutic milieux have to be created as physical and organizational entities by people who have a global concept of their value and the energy and expertise to get them off the ground. As we shall see later, this exercise, and the fact that the need for such a milieu to be supported, housed, staffed, and administered, brings into the situation factors that often militate against the successful creation of a therapeutic community or environment.

In brief, therapeutic communities are institutions that are set up, designed to allow the residents of that community the freedom to create a therapeutic situation based on the assumptions outlined above. That is, one that encourages equality of status and thus the use of all the resources of knowledge, skill, and feeling that exist within the community by sharing; by creating a community where it is recognized that there are as many paths towards participation and involvement as there are people involved, and that to generate any preferred form of approach would be to cut off all those who found they could not conform; but yet to have an organization in which the members were constantly faced with the reality of their behaviour, its consequences and effects; and, finally, in which all possible lines and methods of communication are held open for use.

Like all assumptions about human behaviour, especially those related to the effecting of change, concentration upon a preferred theme institutes a certain degree of blindness. Therapeutic communities do have rules of behaviour, they do expect conformity to the ethos of the institution; power is not equal nor is status conceived to be so. Resistance to the dependency state must curtail the freedom of some to choose what they would wish.

Whenever there is some definite concept of how maximum benefit will accrue, there must also be some definite ideas of what is counterproductive. Even where the group controls in an essentially democratic way, that group has been initiated into that process and the structure established by the exercise of power. The residue of that power lies in the organization's acceptance and continued use of that method of procedure and inevitably is perceived so to exist by all those taking part.

Within the therapeutic milieu, as in most other human groupings, conformity is equated with security and some satisfaction. The final basic assumption that such institutions make is that the insight engendered within its confines, the learning about behaviour, attitudes, feelings, and responses will remain with each participant when he or she leaves, not as a pleasant memory but as usable and integrated knowledge. However, there is some difficulty here analagous to psychoanalysis and psychodelic experiences, i.e. therapeutic milieu experience is not directly communicable to others, it is a personal adjustment that has to show indirectly if at all. Thus, the learning is essentially personal, barely quantifiable except in subjective assessment form, and often a fairly delicate implantation that requires some considerable and constant nurturing if it is to survive the onslaught of the conformity-exacting pressures of the larger society. Practitioners say that what has been gained, in insight, say, can never be wholly lost because it *has happened.* It may revert to the status of a memory rather than that of a driving motivation to behaviour, but at least an experience of what is possible has been lodged when no such experience previously existed and it can, and does, have some influence on post-experience behaviour however minimal.

We must now look at how the design of therapeutic communities can maximize first the experience; second, the take-up rate, and, third, the transfer of the experiential learning to performance modification.

Design possibilities

'Indeed, perhaps paradoxically, one of the issues which becomes apparent from comparisons between the various contributions is the importance of relating a design to its particular therapeutic goals and activities, which typically involves a careful characterisation of the particular patients. At present there appears to be a great deal of confusion as to the nature and value of environments designed for therapy.'

(Canter and Canter 1979 : 2)

What an analysis of the design of therapeutic environments and communities tends to reveal is the somewhat depressing fact of the strength of existing constraints to nullify or reduce the effect of design factors. But this has to be examined much more closely rather than left as such a general negative statement. There is a strong implication otherwise that no matter what design factors are taken into consideration, the outcome will be determined by elements of the situation that cannot be controlled. This is just not true.

The crucial element is relation to context. Groups in which the design is related to the desire to create a milieu most conducive to some avowed aim, and in which the design elements relate only to the ingroup organization are, barring fortunate accidents, notoriously unsuccessful. The reason is not difficult to find. As has been said many times, no group exists in a vacuum. It is part of a supra-system and is itself composed of sub-systems. It is part of a continuous chain of interlocking systems all of which influence and are influenced by each other. However, there is a hierarchy of power so that the larger systems tend to influence their smaller constituents more than the smaller influence the larger. This is not universally true and some authorities, notably Mann (1967), hold that the major directional influence in some groups is the sub-groups that form within the larger group. In fact, sub-groups do often form expressly for the purpose of influencing the larger group, but they are not likely to be all that successful unless most of the high-status members of the larger group either agree with the sub-group's aims or are part of the sub-group. The change of direction or emphasis has to be within the tolerance of the larger group even if the limits of that tolerance are wider than has ever been acknowledged publicly.

As Canter and Canter suggest, 'any design solution can only be effective if it relates to a particular context' (1979 : 331). Thus, the information about the 'factors-affecting' deriving from the study of small groups is very relevant to the design of therapeutic environments, especially the factors that have been called constraints.

There are several possible approaches to the question of design, all based on a fairly exhaustive analysis of the 'factors-affecting' that exist in a given or potential situation. Given that the major function of a therapeutic environment is to enhance the effectiveness of the therapeutic endeavour, then the first approach is based on a reduction or destruction of inhibiting factors in so far as this is possible. The problem here is that the creation of a therapeutic environment tends to bring into conflict situations that did not previously exist, e.g. administrators cannot react badly to an organization that does not exist except in argumentative form. When it is in existence then actions that go counter to the unit's interests can actually take place. Of course, they might be predictable but often they are not, because what looked acceptable as an idea may become largely unacceptable in reality.

As designers have neither prescience nor a crystal ball, and nor is there a great deal of previous experience to go on, then unforeseen problems of this nature are almost bound to arise. However, the ability to predict snags in the therapeutic endeavour and plan them out, is the most frequently used approach, particularly where the new venture is an extension of, or an addition to, an existing system.

Another design approach is to attempt to create a new and different system. This implies that not only the immediate unit being created must be designed, but also the supra-system in which it is embedded. In this sense the designers are attempting not just to take cognizance of the context in which the unit will exist, but to create it on their own favourable terms. Of course the creation has to stop somewhere and where it makes contact with the existing situation, the hope is that the periphery of contact is far enough away from the core effort for what lies outside that boundary to have a filtered effect on the therapeutic endeavour. One way often tried in this category is the development of the self-supporting foundation, or alternatively the physical removal of the new creation from the sources of influence from which it is essential it should be more or less free.

In all matters of design where the crucial function is to provide an enhanced performance, whatever the course taken, its success seems to be directly related, as in sensitivity training groups, to the ability of the designers to bring into the open all, or most of, the factors that will affect the outcome. 'The art of the possible' describes succinctly what design is all about. This is difficult enough under the best circumstances, it is often relegated to near oblivion by those whose enormous enthusiasm for a particular therapeutic approach causes them to attempt to dismiss all apparent obstacles. Environments created to embalm a particular function or idea are nearly always enormously lacking in support for other facets of existence that are equally, if not more, important than that which is apparently of paramount importance. Hospitals are a good example of how the physical environment is designed to facilitate the therapeutic endeavour and the management of people. It tends to precipitate psychological problems, destroys a large element of privacy, generates fear in patients by its formality, and promotes the loss of the ability to direct one's life, no matter how successful it may be in achieving its primary objective.

In this instance, the design concentrates on the facility of treatment and disregards the whole person. This is an incredibly forceful demonstration of power and powerlessness that may mitigate against the therapeutic endeavour by the generation of resistance, fear, and excessive difficulty in readjustment to changed circumstances. Too many severe changes in life style are very destructive of the human being's ability to cope (see Rahe 1972; Holmes and Rahe 1967).

Improvement in the design of therapeutic environments is obviously possible, but one of the essential ingredients of success is a global understanding of the intermeshing of possible influence factors in the existing situation, and a reasonable forecast of what might change, and how, when the design is implemented.

Problems

'A member of staff in a senior position within a so-called therapeutic community was confronted in an administration meeting, because of the lack of discussion, over a decision taken mechanically. He defended himself by saying, "I can't listen to every Tom, Dick and Harry". The essence of a truly therapeutic community is precisely that "Tom, Dick *and* Harry" all have an absolute right to be heard.'

(Maré and Kreger 1974 : 57)

As we have seen, therapeutic environments while being specifically planned, are often founded upon minimal evidence of the effectiveness of the design elements used. When we look at the problems of therapeutic environments and communities here, we must bear this fact in mind. Discovering what has gone wrong does not imply that the basic concept of designing to meet known needs is wrong, it is more likely to tell us that first we did not know what design elements best met given needs and, second, the evidence for effectiveness is slight or non-existent, not because it cannot be discovered, but because few have thought it necessary to look for it.

Without doubt, one of the major problems, which is directly related to lack of information about design elements, is the over-estimation of the resources and capabilities of component factors. Take just the human element. The successful running of a therapeutic community is dependent to an undiscovered but obviously large degree upon the belief that the members have in the efficacy of this form of community. To make it work they must subscribe to the dogma on which the community is founded. But, as the Maré and Kreger quotation shows, the strain of performing such a dedicated role is often too much, and the solid, united presentation of role-modelling behaviour, which is after all for most people an adopted role based upon a rational decision to behave so, is broken into by personal responses.

What this shows, irrespective of the size or importance of the lapse, is that the behaviour is a stance, i.e. it is artificial in the sense that it is created for a specific, rationally selected outcome. It is not, as it were, natural, and can quite clearly be seen as an 'influence' attempt. Probably one reason why religious communities are so much more successful in this aspect of community life is that their members behave as they do because to do so is a natural and readily accepted affirmation of a commonly held 'natural' desire. In other words, the strain of constant role-playing to achieve significant ends is much diminished both by the unanimity of belief and by acceptance of the 'living together' syndrome as falling well within the natural behaviour patterns.

Another prime problem is that of the 'environing supra-system'. Ellis *et al.* (1978) write that any form of group can only be truly understood in relation to the next higher level of organization in which it is set, the so-called 'environing supra-system'. The Canters (1979) write 'we are arguing that the potential for great improvement in therapeutic settings is available, provided the changes which are made are done so in the knowledge of the complexity of the processes which they are housing and of the complexity of the administrative framework which has to accommodate them'.

Clearly the Canters are talking about insufficient cognizance being taken of the 'factors-affecting'. In the 'natural' groups analysed earlier, the great disparity of use of these factors has arisen because over very long periods of time it has been demonstrated which are the most essential for procuring successful outcomes. Likewise, such groups demonstrate that given the irremovable or unmodifiable existence of certain factors, boundaries are thereby set to what is achievable, and to try to flout such constraints is to court some degree of disaster. Time and again the Canter's review of research on designing therapeutic environments shows how the administrative structure in which the therapeutic experiment is embedded, its environing supra-system, can take over and modify, sometimes drastically, the therapeutic aims for which the experiment was originally created.

Thus what has been called the over-idealization of the method has resulted in insufficient weight being given to constraining factors. This applies not just to the supra-system but also to the physical structure of the therapeutic environment and to the human element. Of these the physical, material structure is the easier to deal with. Perhaps because so much more is known about the psychological effects of physical environments and that bricks and mortar, space, colour, furniture and furnishings, lighting, heating, and ventilation are practical realities, too much is often built into their effect or expected from it. After all, a long-standing tradition exists about the design and construction of buildings for explicit purposes. But these buildings have often been for private or business use and the people that use them are the people who agree the design. This does not apply to many existing buildings containing therapeutic facilities designed to accommodate and facilitate the work of the professional staff. It is their assumptions about what their clients want that constitute all the coverage usually given to the facility-users for whom, in theory at least, the building exists.

But, as we have seen, the qualities of the members of any group are a powerful constraint on its performance. To ignore the members of the largest sub-section of any organization and to deny them consultation on the grounds that the smaller professional sub-group can adequately represent their interests as a spin-off of ensuring their own, is to create an enormously clear non-verbal signal of the powerlessness of the larger group. This is hardly a propitious element in a therapeutic environment.

Like all organizations, therapeutic communities and environments need constant reappraisal, a self-reviewing mechanism. In the current state of knowledge about design elements it must be a totally unrewarding exercise to believe that the design could be correct at the first go. There are the wear and tear on staff, the techniques used, the emerging but unforeseen problems, especially those that the organization itself has generated, the time factor, the reappraisal of necessary skills and many other factors that can only be guessed at in the planning stage. Constant checks are necessary to see what is actually happening, e.g. where ossification is setting in as protective device.

Therapeutic environments work by virtue of creating a milieu in which as many factors as possible are controlled to maximize beneficial effects. The overall effect is one of response to the behaviour of others and allowances have to be made for the expectations that people have of the community or environment before they enter it. There is so much to consider and so little evidence of what the weighting of each factor should be. The Canters say that no general proposed design solutions are available, but a series of key questions for designers are. They list the following:

1 Is a special environment necessary?
2 Can therapeutic processes be set in motion by changes in physical surroundings?
3 Are there aspects of the therapeutic process that are being undermined by the designation, utilization, or modification of spaces?
4 Does the provision of this facility in this location tend to make it part of a larger setting or does it help to establish it as a smaller unit?
5 Does this facility have the administrative autonomy that is most effective for stimulating staff attitudes towards therapeutic processes?
6 Are there some appraisal processes that we ought to set in motion in order to find out clearly the nature of our current environmental state?
7 Are the details of the provisions in the physical setting appropriate for the goals of that setting?

(Canter and Canter 1979 : 335–40)

The basic idea of the therapeutic community is a good one, but the problems of running such a community are not well understood. In fact, some of the problems may only just be emerging as therapeutic communities exist for some time – they are self-generating problems.

11

SPECIFIC TYPES OF 'CREATED' GROUPS

INTRODUCTION

'Broadly speaking the aims of those who are concerned with the application of group theory to everyday life are of three kinds – 1. the easing of human relations; 2. the enrichment of human personality; 3. getting people to do things they would not otherwise do. These aims frequently overlap, but it is convenient to deal with them separately.' (Sprott 1958 : 187)

One of the main arguments for the use of groups specifically created to achieve certain ends has been that as group influence generated behavioural patterns in the first instance, they should therefore prove to be the most effective method of changing them. This is what Sprott was discussing in category 1 in the quotation above. So groups have been created in many walks of life in order to change behaviour. But this is quite obviously not all. Groups are equally good at maintaining existing patterns of behaviour by giving confirmation to them and also at moving people to further effort in the same direction. Given that a group has been in existence long enough to develop a reasonable level of trust, it becomes very supportive of the commonly held views. Each member can withstand attack on these views, confident in the knowledge that he or she does not stand alone, and can advance supported by his or her allies. This is Sprott's category 3.

Third, a group is a resource pool that is greater in any given area than the resources possessed by any single member. However, a problem exists in that for a variety of reasons these resources are often enough never used to the full. The main reasons are that they are never made explicit and therefore are not recognized as existing. Also, lack of trust may retard any offer of a resource to the group by any of the members, and traditional methods of operating may ignore what resources do exist because no one ever thinks of asking for them to be used.

Fourth, groups facilitate learning about group behaviour, about others, about oneself, and about co-operative effort. Thus, the four main uses to which groups may be put can be listed as:

1   An instrument of behavioural or attitudinal change.
2   An instrument of support and maintenance.
3   A pool of resources.
4   An instrument to facilitate learning.

Item 3 is obviously different in kind from the others in that it describes what a group has to offer whereas the others describe what it can do.

The selection of which part of the resources of a group is used to achieve any particular end is a crucial factor in efficient group use and leads to a myriad apparently different kinds of created groups all stressing particular features. In this section I want to look at groups designed to produce change, and support programmes, and at those that generate learning.

If the people who create these kinds of groups have learned anything from groups that have arisen traditionally to meet given social needs, then these 'designed' groups will show the designer's intention in the selection and use of the design elements.

GROUPS THAT ATTEMPT TO ACHIEVE CHANGE IN PEOPLE

'Group workers typically serve groups that exist over extended periods of time . . . the worker's task is to influence the course of a group's development so that it permits maximum attainment of the treatment goals set for the participating clients.'

(Vinter 1967 : 63)

Working on the basic assumption that group influence was largely responsible for shaping the individual, it is not hard to see why it should be suggested that groups should be created to use exactly the same kind of influence process to bring about desirable change. Many people when faced with crisis in their lives, or when reviewing the cumulative effect of their life for one reason or another, are often disappointed with some part or even with much of what stands revealed. Behavioural patterns, habits, attitudes, beliefs, opinions, and responses to others tend to be unsatisfactory to the point of being disruptive of social life, handicapping, disorganizing, or even destructive. Thus change, defined as movement to a more agreeable and acceptable quality of living, becomes an urgent and desirable necessity.

Psychotherapeutic groups are one form in which the basic aims are concerned with effecting just such a change. Foulkes and Anthony (1957) listed the aims of their form of group psychotherapy as:

1 To provide relief through expression and catharsis.
2 Restoration through participation and acceptance.
3 The laying bare of disturbing conflicts bringing them into awareness.
4 The liquidation of old fixations in development and the liberation of creative forces in the individual.

Yalom (1970) had a somewhat longer list of aims:

1 To impart information.
2 To instil hope.
3 To demonstrate universality and altruism.
4 To produce a corrective recapitulation of the primary family group.
5 To develop socializing techniques.
6 To cause behaviour to be initiated.
7 To generate interpersonal learning.
8 To achieve group cohesiveness and catharsis for the members.

Now these are aims for a group established on the basis of the group designer's belief that the problems for which these aims are the corrective are themselves the original problem. In other words, analysis of the problems is rooted in the particular theoretical account of behaviour and of human beings that the designer holds. But even so, whatever his or her fundamental belief about human beings, and so whatever tasks he or she requires the designed group to perform, he or she still has a limited number of design elements to use.

Is there evidence, then, that the use of the design factors known to promote the effects required by the group creator are much used in practice? Sadly, the answer must be no. Beyond the traditional methods passed on from teacher to pupil, no really serious analysis exists of why these methods work and others do not.

Smith, Wood, and Smale (1980), in an analysis of the usefulness of groups, noted the following:

Group psychotherapy with children	Significant effects are quite frequently obtained; no preference of one method over another.
Group psychotherapy with severely disturbed patients	Sometimes has a marked effect on adjustment. More substantive changes are not achievable within the format of therapy groups meeting so briefly.
Group psychotherapy for neurotics	With specific behaviour problems it may well be that brief forms of group behaviour therapy can be effective. With general anxiety disorders it is less likely to be positive.

If we now take Yalom's (1970) list and attempt to show what the 'factors-affecting' each of the aims might be, perhaps a clearer picture will emerge of the group that might achieve these aims.

Impart information	A resource function of leader and members. The leader obviously

	can impart information from the start of the group and members can do so when they feel safe to share with others.
Instil hope	Hope is not easily instilled by verbal exchanges but by the perception of the members that change is possible, depending on the degree of hopelessness that pre-existed the group. Instilling hope by a growing recognition of the possibility of change and the supportive nature of the group is often a long-term process easily set back by difficulties.
Universality	Arises from hearing and feeling the experience of others. It can start quite early in the group's life, but requires the process of sharing, which, in turn, is dependent upon a relevant sense of security. This is time-related and dependent upon the setting up of a cohesive state, of supportive norms, and on role modelling by the leader.
Altruism	The need to help others can only arise when clarification of their problems and difficulties has taken place.
Creative recapitulation of the primary family group	An analysis of the influence of the family group requires the skilled resource of the leader and is related in some sense to the information input. The characteristics of the leader

and the leader-acts are very important here as is the degree to which members are prepared to pursue public conformity or accept privately what is being offered.

Develop socializing techniques

This is very dependent on the existence of norms plus the addition of sanctions. It also requires high levels of inter-action, a supportive milieu in which confrontation has a ben-eficial rather than a harmful outcome.

Cause behaviour to be imitated

Role modelling is a norm-making procedure. Time is necessary for even ground rules of behaviour to be established by feedback.

Generate inter-personal learning

Interaction at a high level with meaningful outcomes, high satisfaction levels, feedback, and discussion.

Achieve group cohesiveness

Minimally takes about twelve hours of member contact. It requires much discovery inter-action and development of predict-ability of responses; security plus attraction is a time-related phenomenon.

Catharsis

Emotional discharge also requires the development of relevant security.

Without question the principal design element in the psycho-therapeutic group Yalom had in mind is time. Some factors among the aims are almost contradictory. Factors 1, 5, and 7 require directly the strong, directive, charismatic leader. Most of the others require enabling leadership which generates a group that is a unit and aware of its resources. The directive leadership functions are not time-related, the others are. Almost inevitably, therefore, any success achieved in this kind of group would be dependent upon the charisma, knowledge, and skill of the leader, which explains the brevity of life of such groups, noted by Smith *et al.* (1980), and the not very high level of significant effects.

In a word, the balance of good and bad design factors for the outcome required produces only marginally effective groups. Groups that aim to produce such a group-cohesive, supportive entity should not be leader-focused and should have ample time in which to grow into the kind of option-based or shared experience that can trust and can use its own resources.

Whiteley and Gordon, quoting the evidence from many sources as part of their evaluation of group psychotherapy, write:

> 'Empirical evidence from group psychotherapy research corroborates the group dynamic literature, which emphasizes the significance of group cohesion . . . well developed groups should be maintained not only through successive phases of treatment but if possible during the difficult period of community readjustment. Criteria for determining compatible groups should be used in selection procedures.'
>
> (Whiteley and Gordon 1979 : 199)

This is a plea as much for the correct use of time as for the design elements of cohesion and selection.

Not all groups designed to bring about change are psychotherapeutic in nature.

GROUPS THAT ATTEMPT TO MAINTAIN STABILITY OR SUPPORT

Most groups contain some element of support for their members. But the basic function of groups specifically designed to be supportive and maintaining must be to ensure not just an atmosphere that envelops members, but also one that enhances the use of the group's total resources. Resource-exploitation for the benefit of all the group members is a characteristic clearly visible in self-help groups. So, if we look at the aims of such a group they should serve as an example of all support group systems.

Killilea (1976:178) gives the aims of self-help groups as attempting to use:

1 The common experience of members.
2 Mutual help and support.
3 The 'helper' principle.
4 Differential association (mutual reinforcement).
5 Collective will-power and belief.
6 Importance of information.
7 Constructive action towards shared goals.

Thus a group whose main aim is to support its members, employs the processes and 'factors-affecting' that elicit the common ground of members in the same way that friendship groups do. Similarity becomes the major attraction because it implies understanding not just at the level of knowledge but also of experience. Moreover, having survived such experience, other members are something of a guarantee that survival is a possibility and indeed a probability.

Similarity of problem, of behaviour, or of difficulty also implies some dissimilarity in methods of coping. One of the principal resources of support groups after experiential understanding is the technique of coping that offers others a chance to replace their deficient coping patterns with those found relatively more effective by others.

What groups of this nature need in their design is a combination of factors, e.g. to select for similarity of problem and also for difference of attempts to cope with it, to bring such people together under circumstances that can lead to a group forming with sufficient basic trust to be able first to share, second to use their combined resources, and third, to emphasize not their dependence upon others but their growing ability to support themselves. Such a combination requires an individual or small group to set things going, collect members, establish ground rules of behaviour, and encourage interaction so that shared experience can lead to increased satisfaction, to safety, and to a degree of freedom to share resources.

It is not surprising that such groups are among the most successful of groups created for specific purposes. Because members' needs are clear and the means of meeting them within a group situation are equally clear, this results in a bold and simple group design. Often the problem area is a vital one and motivation is equally high because a level of satisfaction is more readily obtainable due to the low-satisfaction starting point. One great danger is that as success arrives it tends to reduce the motivation to continue in the support group, which can result in a premature disconnection from the system.

The only specialist knowledge and skill required are in the leader who establishes the group in the first instance and lays down the guidelines for its future conduct. Significantly, leadership skills in the setting-up phase are different from those required at later stages in all groups but never more so than in a resource group. Essentially, the skill lies in creating the group, setting it on course, allowing it to develop, enrolling new members, and saying farewell to old ones. The resource is the group at all stages after its inception not the leader.

'The groups which offer most to their members are those which manage to combine mutual support for those who share a common problem with projects which enable people to build up a new set of relationships.' (Robinson in Smith 1980 : 184)

Robinson highlights the final factor in the success of support groups, what he calls 'projects'. The members take from the group not only the psychological support of similarity or commonality, but also levels of knowledge and, often enough, practical experience that is almost immediately usable in life outside the group. This is no mystic experience, but hard factual data and experience shaped to the central problem. This is often accompanied by a much clearer appreciation of how the particular problem has become self-perpetuating.

GROUPS THAT ATTEMPT TO ENHANCE LEARNING

'A good deal of measurable change does occur after groups, but there is a substantial fade-out of these effects in subsequent months.' (Smith 1980 : 46)

As far as experiential groups are concerned, Blumberg and Golembiewski (1976) see learning and change as occurring together. They quote Bennis's (1962) formulation of the meta-goals of laboratory education:

1 Expanded consciousness and recognition of choice.
2 A spirit of enquiry.
3 Authenticity in interpersonal relations.
4 A collaborative conception of the authority relationship.

Perhaps the major differences between a group designed to enhance learning and the 'support' group we have just been looking at are first an increase in complexity of design and, second, an aim not to deal with a common problem but to attempt to reach the central being of any person, whether or not they apparently have a problem.

In essence, these groups are concerned with what Golembiewski and Blumberg (1970) call the process of 'learning how to learn'. The first part of this process is to learn an entirely different method of learning from that normally associated with school. The responsibility for the learning process thus becomes the burden of the individual group member who begins to understand that no expert authority is going to offer answers to the questions he or she wants to ask. The group has to learn how to tolerate ambiguity because certainties are infrequent and expectations have to be explored rather than met.

Probably the most important element of this kind of group, and one that encloses all the other factors, is that the group usually contains, or has access to, most of the resources that members will need in order to facilitate their learning. After all, the main resources are the group and its dynamics and the resources the individual members bring into it. These can best be used when the group is somewhat isolated from everyday life, which is why most such groups meet in residential settings. Also, because time is an important factor, the residential scene increases the value of the span of time that members spend in each other's company, and more quickly brings up the point where shared experience creates predictability and thus an element of trust.

It is no accident that while such groups are successful in their attempts to generate learning, their overall success in changing behaviour patterns is not very remarkable. In the first place there is a degree of ambiguity about what exactly the group is attempting to achieve and an element of essential vagueness about what processes really bring about such aims as exist. For instance, developing 'increased skill in relating to others' is not the clearest of purposes, and even the 'personal growth' movement, which emphasizes the development of awareness about oneself, is not precise. Yet significantly it was because it became so much more precise that the exponents of personal growth groups could become much more specific about the processes that affected their desired outcome, and so design much tighter programmes as a result, including exercises and games.

Nevertheless, both kinds of groups tend to develop what Smith (1971) calls 'little Utopias, painfully constructed but beautiful to be in'. How far such groups bring about private acceptance as opposed to public conformity is a moot point and thus the transferability of learning becomes an uncertain outcome. The experience that such groups create is of a mini-society in which the accepted rules of behaviour are changed to permit members to live a transient existence that places a premium upon honesty, sincerity, and sharing. In a supportive net, individual members can expose and learn about themselves from the verbalized and acted-out response of others. They can become perceptive about relationships, and experience the purging effects of disclosure.

But they are doing these things in a society that not only protects and supports but also creates a norm in which such behaviour is highly acceptable. The learning that comes from such a situation is real and often enough is lasting, but it seems to endure more in the form of knowledge of what is possible in a secure situation than become an influence on ordinary everyday behaviour. Without doubt, learning groups generate a situation in which conformity brings great rewards, not least because they are quite painfully arrived at. But we know that conformity needs sustenance, it needs support and nurturing from positive feedback given in an encapsulating system with special norms. As a rule, society does not supply such a system. It does offer feedback that is often negative and destructive rather than positive and able to sustain much personal growth.

The reality of the 'back-home' support system may be the most crucial element in the success or failure of the learning group. Smith (1971) refers to the need for constant reinforcement by going for yet another group experience in much the same way that an addict supports his or her life style by another fix.

This is not to deny that the design of learning groups creates quite considerable growth in knowledge. Members of such groups are exposed to information about behaviour, their own and others, to knowledge of how the group is operating, and to an analysis of how group dynamics are affecting everything. Most members can take this kind of learning away with them in the form of increased understanding. In many minor ways this may affect their life style, but, as has been argued many times here, for large and permanent change to take place, that change would need to have been seen not only as necessary, but desirable, achievable, rewarding, and sustainable.

Selection also plays a large part. Members of learning groups with particular personalities seem to get little from the situation:

> 'Experience seems to indicate that those people whose needs for structure and authority are very high and rigid do not seem to find the experience of much worth.'
>
> (Golembiewski and Blumberg 1970 : 13)

The thrust of learning groups has been to counter the idea that modern Western society undervalues personal relationships in all walks of life, personal, business, and public. The design of learning groups effectively generates experience of rewarding personal relationship experiences, enhances personal awareness and increases understanding of the way groups influence behaviour. The problem is that the design does not, and indeed cannot, without becoming permanent, sustain much of the learning that takes place.

CONCLUSIONS

This section has considered some of the groups, environments, and communities designed to cope with a few of the problems prevalent in Western society. Two major factors and several smaller ones would seem to me to emerge from this brief survey.

First, insufficient attention appears to have been paid to the lessons of combining the elements of group dynamics in a given design so that they function positively to facilitate the aims for which the organization was set up. Second, and arising out of the first point, most of these organizations are a good deal less effective than they could be because the boundaries imposed by some of the group processes are scarcely thought about and they thus exact quite a toll in terms of failure. I should like to examine this positive/negative effect briefly.

Where residential institutions are concerned, the enormous range of situations to which they are applied as a remedy, and the equally enormous range of possibilities that exist within them, make it more or less certain that they will be successful in some areas and in some possibilities. Take prisons for example; they are remarkably successful custodial institutions. The simple fact that they are, with the possible exception of some open prisons, exceptionally difficult to get out of, means that they are successful in keeping criminals away from the rest of society. But they are not successful in changing the behaviour of prisoners to anything like the same degree. For example:

'A former Home Office researcher Sue Fairhead, described her work on persistent petty offenders which showed that many homeless and unemployed men with poor social contacts ended up in prison because *there was nowhere else to go.*

Many were initially picked up for drunkenness but ended up in prison for non-payment of fines.'

This emerged at the British Psychological Society meeting in London on 21 December, 1981. Also quoted at the meeting was a statement by Trevor Bennett that burglars accepted the fact of prison as an inevitable consequence of their activities. In fact, one in ten thought prison life was better than life outside. There is more evidence here of the failure of prison as a change agent than there is of its success.

One of the major reasons for this abysmal failure must be placed squarely on an insufficient understanding of the effect of the powerful support system that prisoner-culture provides, of the sheer destruction of influence attempts caused by the absolute difference created by the two cultures, and the enormous pressures to conform to the prisoner-culture that are placed on any new entrant to the system. The latter is bound to be more effective because friendship groups are effective, because there is a closeness of behaviour patterns, a similarity of status, and of background, and, above all, a common threat from an opposing powerful element of the system. This is a survival situation and even people with great differences in normal circumstances can become co-operative allies in the face of a common threat if sufficient recognition of their common cause exists or can be created.

Basically, the efficacy of any attempt to change (that is, ameliorate) an organization (e.g. prisoner-culture) tends to be trapped by the belief in the system possessed by those operating it and their skills. This is common to all therapeutic communities. There is abundant evidence that the imposition, or even the agreed introduction of different regimes nearly always ignores two prime dynamics of groups. First, changes in the structure of a system are a clear non-verbal communication of where the real power in the system lies and ignores the findings that group members are only truly committed to a structure or a system when they know that they have some ability to influence it at all stages. This applies to those who operate the system as well as those who are operated by it. Where such evidence of powerlessness is accompanied by no possibility of opting out physically, then one of the major probable responses is to create a counter-vailing system that will render the main system ineffective by non-co-operation (see, for instance, Douglas 1976 : 99–106). Obedience may well occur that is conformity in public, but private acceptance does not, and cannot, follow, because no desire for change has been engendered. On the contrary, all the press-ures are to the confirmation of existing attitudes, a reaffirmation of loyalty to the group which offers more and better satisfaction of needs. The design of most, but not all, residential institutions places in the hands of the residents the best instruments to maintain their current behaviour and beliefs and to resist change.

Let us now consider the second point. All groups as systems are embedded in larger groups, supra-systems. All members of groups are members of other groups even though they can only be physically present in one group at any one time. The influence of the other group is always present, or at least always available. Where groups are designed to use group pressures to bring about change, or growth, or support, it is clear that this can only be done with safety and efficiency in a group that has become a source of great satisfaction to its members.

One of the major factors in the prison groups is the inability of the members to withdraw, except psychologically, from a system that applies pressure wholly dissonant with the satisfactions it provides. Therapeutic groups start with the advantage of a relatively clear need on the part of the members that the group might well be able to meet. But the snags here can be illuminated by two factors: first, the principle of embedding, and, second, the element of time.

Embedding only shows up when a system, i.e. a group, which is part of a larger system, tries to create for itself patterns of behaviour that are manifestly incompatible with the accepted and acceptable behaviour patterns of the larger system. Now, if these new patterns create goods for the larger system, the change may be tolerated because the cost-effective system is still in credit. But, if it should not create goods, then the supra-system will tend to render the group's outcomes unattainable. By demonstrating the group's overall powerlessness in important matters and its impotence, the supra-system will confine the group to boundaries within the accepted range.

It has been said that group influence only really works when a group has actually been created, that is, when a group has 'formed'. This often takes a long time because members have to learn that the group can reward them for their loyalty to it in some very tangible way. And it takes time before members are willing to take risks to see how well they will be supported. This supportive factor can be accelerated by skilled group leadership, but more often than not a powerful, charismatic leader approach is adopted because the time taken to achieve results can be lessened by directive leadership. The satisfaction of the members is then related not so much to their membership of the group as to their dependence upon, and trust in, the leader.

But whereas the group, had it developed as such, might have enhanced the members' ability to understand the group's pressures and their own responses, the transfer of learning from the directive leader situation is much less readily undertaken. The dependent state is that much more difficult to convert because in a very real sense the learning it involves has not grown from within but has been imposed from without. The resource for the learning has been an external factor, not an internal one.

It is no accident that most therapeutic groups attempt some form of segregation to engender a closer affinity between members and reduce the effect of other influences by intensifying contact. To cut off other sources of stimulation creates a situation in which the existing group becomes the only available supply system; it enhances the apparent satisfaction that the group can give and thus engenders an increased sense of belonging. There is no doubt that this sense of belonging is real. There is equally no doubt that such experience can open members' eyes to the possibility of change. The crunch comes when this protected state ceases to exist and the learning and potential have to be continued, developed, and consolidated in a larger and basically uncaring system. The figures available on the maintenance of change are not all that encouraging and show a marked discrepancy between return to a sympathetic, or to an unsympathetic, or apathetic larger system.

Perhaps one of the principal difficulties is loss of interest. Because group-containing systems are set up with enormous enthusiasm but often little clear, data-based understanding of group processes, they do not succeed as their creators expect. This results in apathy and withdrawal, in acceptance of a low level of function as being all that is possible. An increment of understanding might well have prevented such a loss.

Another factor, of course, is cost. The size of units, the proliferation of adequately trained people, and the time involved, all tend to make successful group operations relatively expensive. For instance, even groups that apparently operate at low cost on the basis of self-help have seldom-acknowledged extremely high cost factors in the time and dedication of the founder members, often only realized as such when volunteer workers may have to be replaced by paid workers.

Through its rulers, society will only pay for what it deems to be important and the generally low level of performance of its caring institutions may well reflect the priority system. Of course, the dedication of some individuals (at high cost) can raise the standard of efficacy markedly even in the face of an apathetic public. But my main point is that due consideration of the design factors could make many group operations more effective and thus more cost-effective. If success breeds success then eventually those in need of care could get a better deal with little or no increased cost.

PART FOUR

Implications

INTRODUCTION

'We live in a social environment which is in constant flux.
Much of what happens to us is related to the activities of
groups to which we do or do not belong; and the changing
relations between these groups require constant readjust-
ments of our understanding of what happens and constant
causal attributions about the why and how of the changing
conditions of our life.'   (Tajfel 1969 : 81)

If what I have tried to show so far has some element of truth in it,
then the possible implications for individuals and communities
must be almost endless. How many of the social and personal
problems that seem intractable are so difficult to understand
because they are founded in a kind of group training that is so
well absorbed that its sources are not only lost to the consciousness of those involved but can only be guessed at by those who
observe? How far is it possible to see that often enough it is an
individual who performs but it is his or her 'group training'
experiences that have defined not only the exact circumstances
under which he or she performs but the level, intensity, nature,
and anticipation of the consequences of that performance?

   In their book *Wife-Beating: The Silent Crisis*, Langley and
Levy (1977) show quite clearly that when stress factors lower
consciousness of socially acceptable behaviour patterns, other
patterns, such as wife-beating, emerge that are also socially
acceptable at a most covert level. This second level is tacitly
supported by most men in the community who would probably
publicly express disapproval but privately be unconcerned, secure in the knowledge of general agreement with their stance (all

having been subjected to a similar group training imposed continuously by group pressure).

People tend to analyse their social situations in terms of the values they have learned earlier in their lives when, as Gioscia (1974) says, they are 'young, helpless and uncritical'. Attitudes, beliefs, opinions, and prejudices are all formulated in this way. But the time scale is changing. Whereas it was once possible for the values of grandparents to have salience for their grand-children (and this may in certain essential areas still be so), the speed of social change has accelerated to the point where many of the beliefs and attitudes acquired early in life are woefully inadequate for coping at maturity.

This necessarily leads to a critical examination not only of those attitudes and beliefs, but also of the methods of their creation and absorption so that the process can be used to generate adaptive change. People have now such destructive potential that the maladaptive nature of perceptions produces an ever increasing risk that the human race could be obliterated by what could be termed an error, or series of errors, if any one was left to make such a judgement.

It is the purpose of the last part of this book to take several areas of our social existence and to attempt to indicate that just a moderately enhanced understanding of the way group processes operate and how they ensure given outcomes, could make some appreciable difference to those same areas of life. But this can be but an indication, nothing more. The social problems considered here are often vast with a weighty history of many attempts at understanding and change. My sole purpose is to suggest that perhaps the influence of group factors has either been under-estimated or ignored both in the generation of the problems and in the methods propounded for dealing with them.

Social injustice obviously exists, but what it is depends to a great extent on how the individual has been conditioned to perceive social justice. No matter how much that individual applies the force of reasoning power to a situation to produce a rational analysis of the society in which he or she lives, the power of original patterns of understanding fostered during his or her socialization will still remain very great. This is especially so when his or her rational assumptions are confronted by a situation engendering emotions related directly to his or her early socialization. Then, what passes for rational discussion becomes justification both for a deep-seated emotional response and for a highly conditioned perception of the factors involved.

Of course, many deliberate acts of social tyranny exist: many social situations are generated from greed, spite, and hatred, but the fact remains that such ascribed reasons are not the whole cause and often enough are not even a sufficient explanation.

12

A CONSIDERATION OF SOME
OF THE
MAJOR IMPLICATIONS

'We cannot thereby speak of the meaning of any behaviour. There is instead a system of meanings in broader and broader levels of circumstance and experience. Furthermore, we cannot think of any act as having a meaning of its own, for meaning is not a property of the behaviour itself. The term "meaning" applies instead to a relation of behaviour and context.'   (Scheflen 1974 : 179)

In Scheflen's sense, people are truly social animals. Scheflen is saying that the much vaunted individual nature of human beings is actually so lacking in genuine separateness that it can only be truly understood in its social context. Moreover, that context is not only the milieu that the individual currently inhabits, i.e. at the time of observed behaviour, but extends backwards through the whole of his or her past, providing schemata, references, expectation, and knowledge of possible consequences. Berne (1975) called this kind of programming 'Life-Scripts' and suggested that some knowledge of how the script was written, how it had been modified, and what it currently contained, was a prerequisite of beginning to have choice. By choice Berne meant a conscious ability to select among alternatives, in reasonably adequate knowledge of what they were.

Freudians tend to concentrate exclusively on the historical development of the script; others are more concerned to accept that the past has created the present response patterns and to show the consequences of those patternings in current and future behaviour. Either way, the attempt is to make the mainsprings of behaviour accessible to the individual.

> 'There was a young man who said "Damn,
> It seems to me that I am,
> A being that moves
> In predestined grooves,
> Not a bus, not a car, but a tram".'   (Anon.)

The analogy is not exact because the driver of the tram is well aware that freedom of choice of action in direction and destination is strictly limited by the nature of the vehicle's construction and the track upon which it runs. It is clear that most individuals believe they have a considerable freedom of choice when indeed they are equally as circumscribed as the tram. Too often those who have thought about the restriction imposed on human beings by their nature and nurture, are prone to believe that these restrictions are obvious to all when, in fact, few people give the matter much thought except at such crises in their lives where their lack of self-awareness may be forced upon them. Even then the more likely reaction is self-justification. As Festinger (1957) and others have shown, such a challenge to the individual's long-established belief about his or her own nature produces a state of cognitive dissonance that is not necessarily, or even often, resolved by a movement towards obliterating the difference between the two cognitions of self by an increase in awareness.

Even when the data about interpretation of sensory stimuli are presented, many find it hard to accept the subjective nature of perception; the world is as they perceive it. Kelly's (1955) Personal Construct Theory emphasizes the point that because of this belief in the accuracy of our perception based upon past experience, our worlds are significantly different. When we get past simple data where for various reasons our past has programmed us similarly into the area of feeling, judgement, and so on, our ability to communicate with understanding with our fellow human beings diminishes rapidly and the need for guideposts is sometimes, though never often enough, recognized.

This chapter attempts very briefly to state the implications that group influence has in some key areas of social existence. Sherif (1936) highlighted the pressures exerted on individuals by reference groups. This becomes a fairly unambiguous point at which to start. Reference groups are a generally accepted and acceptable theme; it is a given of their nature that they influence the current behaviour of an individual, often enough without their knowing about it. Indeed such an influence state is often used as an excuse for possible explanations of otherwise inexplicable behaviour.

Then, still in the realm of the acceptable, we look again at group influence in attitudes, opinions, beliefs, and values, and from there we plunge into the maelstrom of conflict and consensus behaviour. We have moved from the 'safe' areas of how behaviour occurs into the quicksands of its occurrence in our society and the phenomenally large traditions of justification that have built up into dogma and belief. The distance from rational understanding as opposed to apparently rational understanding has increased rather dramatically.

Next we look at the social problem of mental illness where the very nature of the problem generates fear and perceptions as widely varied as the traditional concepts of 'madness' and the 'anti-psychiatry' lobby who disbelieve the 'illness' designation of mental disturbance. Here we have to reckon not only with group influence but also with ignorance. It is easy enough to accept the stereotyped responses current in one's social group when one has not been exposed to the real problem or issue to which the stereotype refers. In these matters crisis is often the outcome when coping, e.g. understanding of something, is shown by circumstances to be patently inadequate; a sense of loss tends to accompany this revelation, a sense of dissonance, and a probable potential for change may also be present.

In the section on racialist behaviour, a current social problem of some magnitude is looked at in the light of the analysis put forward here. Finally, in the same terms, we look at decision making and the process of learning.

Any aspect of social behaviour could have been used to demonstrate the insidious working of group pressure; it is all pervading and, I suspect, we are so accustomed to its presence that we no longer see or feel it except when our circumstances change so that some one group pressure or other is highlighted. This occurs when, for instance, we move from one social situation in which we are familiar and at ease to one where we cannot predict the response that our presence and behaviour will elicit. Clearly the unease we feel is related to insecurity and we may become fleetingly aware of how our behaviour has been programmed by our perceptions of the familiar group.

No wonder Goffman (1969) could so convincingly put forward a theory of behaviour that was essentially dramaturgical. We play our parts not only according to our scripts prepared from past response to group experience, but also to our interpretation of our current situation and it is also developed and maintained by our past experience. We are much more tramlike than most of us care to admit, but unlike trams we have the capacity to change if we want to if and when we become aware of our tramlike progress through life.

REFERENCE GROUPS

'Is it really the case that experience itself has become nearly impossible? We think so. Because we become human by learning a set of values, feelings, perspectives and assumptions when we are young, helpless and uncritical. When that set of values and feelings is no longer adaptive to the world we later inherit, we experience a crisis, which commands on the one hand that we interpret the world as we originally learned to do, and on the other that we realise that the world which gave birth to our philosophy is no longer what it was. When we must simultaneously trust and mistrust our most fundamental values, it is hard to know what being human means.'

(Gioscia in Scheflen 1974 : viii)

Reference groups fulfil two major functions: first as a standard of comparison and, second, supplying a pressure towards conformity. Most reference groups fulfil both functions, some one or other functions, and some reference groups are more important to an individual than others so that when there is a conflict from several reference sources over a given issue, the source that dominates has a higher relevance, salience, and priority than the others.

The comparison function links the individual to others who are significant, and who accept him or her, and whose behaviour, attitudes, beliefs, and norms he or she accepts. Such a group forms what Carolyn Sherif calls a 'social anchor'. Using her own life as illustrative material, Sherif goes on to say that she would hold it impossible that anyone could know her without knowing all or most of the social anchors that hold her in her social context.

Reference groups provide individuals with a ready-made instrument for interpreting the world. They eliminate the necessity for making thoroughly investigated decisions about many of the facets of everyday life; they generate a 'socio-centrism' where normality is taken to conform to the standards and values of the reference group. Interestingly, when a reference group exists for an individual, face-to-face contact is not necessary for a continued influence. Only where the social situation changes and an individual is exposed to a new and possibly different reference group does rejection of earlier groups take place, and even then this is seldom an absolute change. Often such individuals find themselves in a kind of limbo, being sure of neither source of reference.

The family is often the most important reference group but others with very strong influence may range all the way from friends, to sub-culture, to nationality. 'People like us' tends to define the sense of belonging and acceptance and to define equally the excluded, the different.

Conformity, which is the second function of the reference group, is a straight exchange of the satisfaction of having roots, of being confirmed as an accepted member for behaving in the appropriate way. This covers attitudes, beliefs, opinions, and feelings. The norms of the reference group dictate much social behaviour, so much so that it is axiomatic that where individuals express a similarity of opinion they usually have common or similar reference groups.

The consequences of this kind of group pressure are manifest. The ability to communicate depends to a large degree not so much on the content of the communication as on the audience perception of the communicator. Credibility tends to rest upon seeing the communicator as belonging to, or being nearly in, one's own reference group. The confrontation that takes place daily between different parts of our society gives a frustrating picture of people who cannot communicate. There is so much evidence that no matter what is said, what words or aids are used, each group is predisposed to discount anything the other says or does. They have different reference groups and mistrust is a norm. Appeals to reason are vain; each implicitly believes his group is reasonable. Each also believes implicitly that his or her group is right and any concessions to the opponents is a generous gesture and not an increasing belief in the veracity of their case. Reference groups affect decision making of all kinds – voting behaviour, for example – choices, judgements, and opinions of all kinds. The inference is clear. No one submits to this kind of control, if they are aware of it, unless the level of rewards for such submission is high.

One of the major problems of our complex society is that for most people the influence of their reference groups is not known to them, at least not directly. It is disguised in clouds of loyalty, tradition, custom, and, above all, in an almost absolute belief that the way things are done is the right and natural way. The fact that few people in our society can be unaware that other social groups do things differently does not seem to have made the impact that might have been expected. Certain peripheral unimportant habits and behaviours pass between social groups, but the basic attitudes and norms that identify individuals with their social group seem to have been reinforced. Other social groups are considered 'funny', or 'peculiar', and strangeness, as always, seems to pose a threat and must be rejected or guarded against.

Work groups are often strong reference groups in that they teach individuals how to behave, show what is expected of them, and give them a code to live by. It becomes increasingly obvious that one of the factors that cohesive work groups develop is a mistrust of other groups. Once again we are faced with the possibility of flexibility and change only in those peripheral areas that are not central or essential to the group.

The fact that much reference group influence is hidden, often unknown to the individual influenced, tends to mean that behaviour emanating from such a source is hardly ever credited to it. Thus, responses to it are misdirected and the element of confusion and mistrust compounded. An understanding of the origins of such behaviour would tend to dictate a different kind of approach probably which used individuals with similar reference group background to communicate, or one that used different experience to create the possibility of new reference groups.

Such approaches are enshrined in peer and self-help groups where similarity of experience creates a common reference and a readiness to accept and be accepted as 'real' which is seldom accorded to the 'specialist'. These are support groups that, over time, become a new reference group for their members and, if the satisfaction of membership is high, may eventually replace old reference groups as a major guiding influence. The diminution of the ability to communicate across social groups can only be changed by an understanding of how it arises in the first place and applying a remedy that operates in the same area of experience.

'There's many an open-necked, ex-working man, his tummy overhanging his jeans, whose utterances are still really aimed at the small group of mates with whom he made it to grammar school; it is they he would have betrayed if he were to join BUPA, buy a tie or give up reading the New Statesman.'

(Whitehorn 1982)

THE FORMATION, MAINTENANCE, AND CHANGE OF ATTITUDES, OPINIONS, BELIEFS, AND VALUES

'Many of our beliefs are due to our unquestioning i.e. un-thinking, acceptance of the beliefs commonly held by the members of our group. Those belonging to other groups will, in the same unthinking way, accept other beliefs concerning some topics.' (Stebbing 1939 : 29)

It has been said that a mature adult has tens of thousands of beliefs, hundreds of attitudes, but only dozens of values. Often enough the distinction between these elements is not made sufficiently clear, largely because the degree of overlap between them is considerable. However, opinions are more transient than attitudes, less salient, and usually much freer of the emotional and evaluative loading found in attitudes.

The main function of these elements is to provide us with keys to make sense of our environment. A second function is to influence our behaviour. They are thus major regulators of behaviour and as such have always had prime interest for social psychologists who have sought to understand how they are formed and how they might be changed. For our purpose how they are created and maintained is of major importance.

All attitudes are learned. Opinions are created from infor-mation and the wholesale adoption from important people in our lives; they are susceptible to change in the light of different information and of change in important relationships. Values tend to be constant, learned early in life, changed seldom except under very significant circumstances, and are very central to the individual personality.

Attitudes are time- and place-linked, initiated by the family, school, and peer groups, and maintained by continued mem-bership of these groups. As we have seen, the family is a very powerful group in that one of its main functions is the socializ-ation of children. In essence this means bringing pressure to bear to mould a child into conforming to accepted patterns of be-haviour prevalent in the society in which the family resides. Now, the salient point here is not what attitudes are actually learned in this system, but that the pattern and style of attitude acquisition has been set. That is, a pattern of acquisition that is dependent upon a state of relative dependence and ignorance coupled with respect and affection and a large element of trust. By the complex process of having to adjust to our environment, attitude acquisition becomes a form of taking over some basic and not so basic instruments of coping, a set of standard answers.

Not only does this process ease adjustment to the society, but it also generates a sense of belonging, in that many attitudes are held in common. That attitudes can, and do, influence behaviour is unquestioned, but the effect is not always direct. Some attitudes would prescribe behaviour that we know would be unacceptable or unfeasible – the attitude persists but the behavioural outcome does not occur, for example, the difference between public conformity and private acceptance.

Attitudes are notoriously difficult to change. They are seldom susceptible to logic, or changed information, or even contradictory experience. Thus, we are faced with possible important influences on behaviour that are not observable, only inferred, and are not accessible to the commoner forms of change attempts. The large element of group pressure that brought about the attitude originally and instigated the process of attitude acquisition and the large emotional element involved are the main reasons for this inaccessibility.

It is no accident that attitudes can most satisfactorily be changed only by simulating the circumstances of their acquisition, i.e. by creating a group with the characteristics previously outlined that can exert sufficient pressure and generate such awareness of the existing attitudes and their consequences that change can come about in security. It is significant that exhortation, pressure, sanctions, and rewards are all relatively unsuccessful in changing attitudes, especially where strong approval or disapproval was a component. Even experience that shows attitudes to be wrong can lead to dissonance that does not necessarily have to be resolved by attitude change, it could be resolved by a rejection of the contradictory experience. There are many implications for our understanding of attitudes and values, and, to a lesser extent, opinions, of the group processes that condition their acquisition and maintenance. In the whole field of social conflict, of apparently entrenched and immovable positions, the attitudes of those involved are of paramount importance.

Sociologists propound three basic concepts of society. One says that all societies work on the fundamental assumption that there is a general consensus, an agreement about the way in which society should function, and that those in disagreement are deviant and should be suppressed. Another says that no society really has this overall agreement but is composed of separate elements whose interests are in conflict with one another. The third concept, which is the inevitable halfway house, proposes that societies are compounds of the first two.

Now, sociologists tend to describe what they see. That is, the social conditions pre-exist the sociologist. But, having been made aware of their conditions as seen by the sociologists, some focus may well be given to discontent among the members of a society or part of a society. The discrepancies in rewards of satisfaction between one group and another are more clearly seen. The realities of power and powerlessness may emerge more forcefully. As the section on attitudes shows, what people use as standards of judgement are largely set by the influence of the groups of which they have been a member.

Membership of a group is maintained by the continued production of acceptable behaviour. This must equally involve rejecting the temptation to non-conforming behaviour and so to the rejection of ideas and beliefs that are contrary to, or even just different from, those held by the group in general. In this way groups, influential groups that is, impose a selective deafness and blindness on their members. Not only do members not accept ideas disapproved of by such a group, they do not actually hear them. Litvak (1967) showed quite clearly how almost impossible it was to get people to hear, let alone accept, views that were not consonant with their own cherished beliefs. Lewin's (1947) classic wartime experiments in changing the food-buying habits of American women, which led eventually to the extreme interest in groups as agents of change, showed that change was associated with a desire to change and was not efficiently generated by exhortation or information giving.

If the group to which an individual belongs is a large one, then it is similarity rather than face-to-face contact that generates loyalty. If all the larger groups within a society have sufficient sense of similarity despite their differences in many other respects, e.g. religion, nationality, or patriotism, then consensus behaviour may be the order of the day. Alternatively, if the whole society is small enough to meet together then the similarity bonding is strengthened by the actual presence of others and majority decisions are obviously possible.

Most large groups no longer seem able to be united by the concept of similarity despite difference, even less than appeared to be the case in the past. So society contains many groups with some similarities but with many obvious points of difference, the former being enough to keep them in society and the latter being large enough to ensure constant conflict. Apart from any aspect of absolute reality that lies behind their differences, people's perceptions of the world they inhabit cause them to believe that their group, and thus their ideas too, must be, in fact are, right. To believe otherwise would be to destroy the foundations on which their world is built. If this generates traditional attitudes towards the wrongness of the ideas held by other groups, and it does as part of the group solidarity, then if such groups come into conflict, the possibility of conflict resolution is considerably diminished by group-reinforced factors have little or nothing to do with the current situation.

This situation is demonstrated in the chapter on work groups where the process of cohesion, i.e. attraction and loyalty to one's work group, was often synonymous with the rejection of other groups. Rejection has to be seen not so much in the negative sense of refusing to accept others as equals, but in the very positive sense of its use as a push against something that compresses or forces together the elements of the group.

Rejection of others is a binding action on the members of a group.

The 'ingroup' and 'outgroup' are expressions not only of belonging but of similarity and difference. The more group A can illuminate to themselves the differences that exist in the members of group B, the more they reinforce their own unity. The more this unity is reinforced, the greater is the power of the group to influence its members, and thus the greater is their belief that the attitudes engendered in their group are right. Not just right in some logical or arguable sense, but right because their rightness is as natural and unquestionably so as the air they breathe.

Such foundations are so strong that logic plays little part in their maintenance or in their change; only personal experience that offers a clearly different interpretation of accepted facts may suffice to do that.

MENTAL ILLNESS

'However impaired physically, the medically ill person can almost always express that he is not intentionally and openly opposing his place in the social scheme of things. So-called mental symptoms, on the other hand, are made up of the very substance of social obligation. Mental symptoms directly express the whole array of divisive social alignments: alienation, rebellion, insolence, untrustworthiness, hostility, apathy, importunement, intrusiveness and so forth. Thus divisive alignments do not – in the first instance – constitute malfunctioning of the individual, but rather disturbance and trouble in a relationship or an organisation.'

(Goffman in Grusky and Pollner 1981 : 199)

If we follow the medical model of explanation for mental illness, we have to accept that mental illnesses are disease entities or hereditary propensities. The most that this model will allow to social circumstances is that they may be precipitating or exacerbating factors. But where is the evidence for this widely accepted thesis? Is it possible to offer unequivocal proof that major mental disturbances arise because the person concerned is ill from some definitely traceable cause? The answer is an emphatic no! The best that can be offered is evidence that some mental states are related very closely with physical trauma, and that mental illness is not a disease of a particular human organ, the brain, but a disturbance of its function.

Laing and Esterson (1970), and Szasz (1961), for example, have suggested that the behaviour of the mentally ill is logical enough given their perceptions of the world in which they live. In a very simple sense it is a withdrawal from a situation in which the individual's perceptions of what constitutes conformity are in conflict with one another, and acceptance from one party or other has always to be balanced against the disapproval and rejection from another of the same element of behaviour. We are now talking about the basic fears of every human being and about group pressure.

Why should we assume quite blithely that when an individual displays bizarre behaviour it is happening because either their functions have suddenly (or slowly) gone awry or, because they were defective in some other way? Why should we postulate sole responsibility to psychological trauma when we accept fairly easily that 'normality' is a response to group pressures demonstrated by an acceptable level of conformity?

The whole mechanism of dislike of difference can be seen in some manifestation of mental illness. Whatever the cause of changes in behaviour, be they physical, or because of biochemistry, damage, illness, or poison, the changes themselves often appear as inexplicable to others. The inexplicable has to have some explanation that can bring it from the unknown into the comfortable sphere of the known, and just such an explanation is concocted. Given the degree of change and its observability, degrees of explanation ranging from eccentric to mad may well be offered. As a consequence, the observers, who are comforted by the thought that explanation of the apparently inexplicable has been given, proceed along the 'as if' programme. That is, they behave towards the individual *as if* he or she were mad. The feedback so given must eventually affect the individual's perception of their own behaviour and their self-image changes accordingly.

Obviously something precipitated change in the first place, but it is the feedback from the groups to which the individual had membership that defines this deviancy in a particular way, and it is the group that responds *as if* this definition were true and finally convinces the individual that they also have an explanation for the unknowable things that are happening or have happened to them.

As the groups that are most involved in this feedback situation are the family, friendship and work groups, it is interesting to note that each of these has strong pressures to conformity and that similarity in two of them is a crucial factor. Something like the way in which an oyster coats an irritant within its body to make a smooth pearl, which is non-irritant, occurs in these group situations. Individual difference of a marked and irritant character that might start to destroy the group by the stark presentation of being unlike is either coated with a socially and culturally acceptable description, which, while allowing for difference, defines it in comfortable terms, or the individual is ejected from the group.

The alternative to ejection immediately exposes the group as weaker than previously; the number of relationship dyads has been decreased by N-1 (N = the number of group members). The resources of the group are diminished not just by the absence of one source, but also by any catalytic or stimulating effect the individual may have had on others. Like the scapegoat of the group, the deviant individual may be of such importance as a group resource that although he or she is reviled and abused, he or she is not actually driven from the group as is the classical scapegoat of Leviticus.

The consequence of this sort of group action is to make the individual who is deemed to be mentally ill an almost inexplicable phenomenon in their individual state, isolated from the milieu in which they are normally embedded without postulating a cause that is equally inexplicable, e.g. 'madness'. History shows that this equation has been used in countless ways and is still used openly in the more primitive societies today. The explanations range all the way from witchcraft, sorcery, and possession, to forms of punishment, and are equally correlated to the normal reality of human beings. All are explanations that offer the group security, an explanation that makes the apparently inexplicable knowable.

Group pressure is not a necessary cause of mental disturbance, though some would dispute this with some justice. Beyond question it is both precipitating factor and an intensifying and confirming agent. The former is achieved through the response difference, the latter through the individual's perception of that response.

ETHNIC GROUPS

'What is the difference between a prejudice and a conviction? In many ways, they are alike. Any conviction worth its salt must be emotionally toned, difficult to change, and selective in its influence on the holder of the conviction. The only clear distinction that seems possible is the fact that the holder of a conviction is psychologically capable of continual re-examination of his belief, while a prejudice cannot be fairly re-evaluated by its owner. Also as we use the term most frequently, prejudices typically are of hostile nature.'

(Levanway 1972 : 328)

Henri Tajfel (Tajfel and Fraser 1978), writing about the 'structure of our views of society', said that, 'the notion of "race" has become *in its general social usage* a shorthand expression which helps to create, reflect, enhance and perpetuate the presumed differences in "worth" between human groups or individuals'.

We have seen that groups are bonded together by very clearly defined characteristics such as the level of satisfaction that the members of any group perceive that the group can offer being high, and greater than the costs of membership. Factors may include proximity, shared experience, a sense of common attitudes, belief, and purpose. But even when most of these are missing, as Runcie (1973) found with the concept of similarity, perceived and recognized similarities are sufficient to bind people into a sense of unity that, although it never actually brings its constituents into face-to-face contact, has some of the major characteristics of 'groupness'.

Similarity implies security; it offers confirmation, it confers a sense of being right, which Aronson (1976) assumes to be such an essential part of human behaviour, and it gives support. All these factors are the positive side of the coin as far as group members are concerned, but, as is always the case, what provides positive gain for one group creates a rather different situation for others. While all these factors are inclusive ones for members, they are exclusive for non-members. Exclusion in this way already asserts difference. Often this is a difference that is totally acceptable and it emerges in behaviour characterized by loyalty on the one hand and competition on the other. But there are other less acceptable consequences.

Berkowitz and Green (1962), and Feldman (1969), for example, have shown that intense personal dislike in groups, which is often the motivation for scapegoating, tends to be focused on members whose difference is both readily seen and salient for the group. For instance, members who are in a minority, expressing caution and hesitation when the group majority is eager to move forward and keen to accept the risks involved, are subjected to an intense barrage of pressure to conform, and their personal esteem in the group is rapidly diminished. Ridicule, an overt expression of dislike, is frequently used as the main instrument of sanction.

If this factor of similarity, and its opposite difference, are placed alongside ignorance of the ways in which people from different cultures behave, we have a potent cause for the generation of apparent difference that may well be increased by clear visual difference in, say, skin colour. That is one side.

On the other side is a clear recognition of difference, plus all those factors concerned with the acceptance into established groups of new members. Even where the similarities are overwhelming, newcomers still have to be accepted, their value to the group proved, and their worth accepted. All newcomers seek points of similarity with those already involved because similarity is not only a powerful binder, it is also apparently the factor that can be stretched to incredibly tenuous lengths and still be a viable bonding agent. Similarity, in race terms, means to a large extent seeking out those of similar ethnic origin as constituting a population that is less different than others. This point is highlighted when people emigrate, but it nevertheless exists in societies that contain citizens of many ethnic origins.

Quite a lot of work on deviance has been shown to postulate a clear relationship between labelling behaviour as deviant because it does not conform to the canons of socially acceptable behaviour and an eventual belief on the part of those so labelled that they are in fact deviant. For whatever reason rules are seen to be broken, the end result is the labelling of the behaviour involved as deviant.

Of course, difference can be operated as a defence. If the members of an ethnic group emphasize their difference to others, not only does this serve to keep their members among the familiar and secure, but it also is a very distinct signal to others to keep out, that they are not wanted, that they are different. All groups that have been together for some time or who have bonds that start them off so far along the path of development of cohesion, tend to respond to outside threat, real or imagined, by a greater binding together for safety and a unitary response from the group as a whole to the perceived threat. Boundaries are sealed and a culture is developed and traditionalized that emphasizes the solidarity of those gathered together.

Obviously the problem is rooted in the similarity/difference factor that is such a potent promoter of groupness (and inclusion) and group conflict (exclusion), which in turn is motivated by the threat posed by perceived difference. If groups of people of identical ethnic background can produce scapegoating behaviour where differences are not openly obvious, then what effort will have to be put into reducing the effects of obvious difference?

This problem has recently been highlighted in this country but it is in no way a new one. Ethnic minorities have always been involved, coming from numerically smaller societies and trying to make their way in the larger society that had the means and opportunities considered desirable. In many cases the more immediate obvious difference lay in the habits of speech – often a totally different language, sometimes a different accent – and in customs, apparel, and religion.

In the larger society, members of ethnic minorities like these not obviously visually distinguishable, form clubs and societies to share their common origins and keep their culture alive in the face of a swamping and alien society. It is often recorded that such groups show a much greater love for their roots when away from them than they ever did when in the area of origin, and when, in fact, their cultural traditions may have been exactly the pressure that drove them to leave in the first place. Group dynamics would lead us to expect exactly that kind of emphasis; the stress would be on the similarity that bonded people together and the difference to those from whom separateness is another form of pressure to bond with one's kin.

Even transient journeys through foreign countries can cause people of the same ethnic group and travelling together to feel more strongly the bonds that unite them, however much they might shun each other's company at home. The clue offered here is the simple one that groups that could unite different peoples would have to cut across ethnic boundaries, but such groups could only exist in two fundamental situations. First, if the level of satisfaction gained by being a member of a multi-racial group was higher in a majority of the more salient aspects of life than any racially pure group, then the loyalty factor would change. This already happens for some in the rewards of the educational system and causes conflict with cultural traditions. Second, if the threat to all those within the larger society was all-encompassing, unity could become an objective promising some reward.

The second situation is group dynamically less feasible than the first, because, as we have seen, to cohere further under perceived threat a group already needs to be a 'formed' group, conscious of its identity and the state of belonging of its members. If it has not achieved this state before the onset of threat, then the responses are individualistic or sub-group based, being largely security-oriented. In such circumstances the component parts of a group frequently use the external threat to gain their own ends at the cost of others, with destruction and disintegration of the larger organization as the end result. It founders in a sea of personal goals that have a far higher priority than the goal of the group's survival as a group. History is littered with examples of such a response to external threat from that of the Greek City States to the immediate past.

DECISION MAKING

'Janis suggested that the members of Kennedy's advisory group were victims of "groupthink", a term that he coined, in keeping with the Newspeak vocabulary of George Orwell's 1984. Janis explained that groupthink is the "deterioration of mental efficiency, reality-testing and moral judgement that results from in–group pressure" (Janis 1972).'

(Raven and Rubin 1976 : 416)

We have seen earlier how the judgement of individuals is affected by the social context in which the need for it arises. Aronson (1976) says human beings have a basic need to be right, i.e. not to be seen to be either ignorant or foolish, a need that relates very closely to the basic fear of isolation, to conformity behaviour, and the desire to be accepted by significant others. Thus most of the available material about decision making is heavily concerned not with the accuracy or efficiency of the decisions human beings make, but with the conscious and unconscious influences that affect the decision making process.

Janis, as quoted above, chose the decisions of major national policy-making bodies in America as his field of investigation. His work was additional to, or perhaps in contrast with, all the earlier work on the so-called risky-shift, which showed that group decisions tended to be riskier than individual decisions. Moreover, the effect of risky decision taking remained with the members of the group as individuals though in a somewhat diminished form when they were no longer involved in direct group influence. There has been much discussion about the influence of groups on decision making, including the evolution of the 'value theory', which postulated a general value for risk-taking in society. Interaction discloses different places on this value scale, the lower ones move upwards and the higher ones downwards, bringing about a general shift in decision taking and also serving to remind members of the generally held value.

Fraser (1978) rightly points out that the existence of such a generalized value scale has never been proved, but the indisputable fact remains that decisions are influenced by the presence of others. This appears to be particularly so if the others involved are respected and their acceptance of each other is a crucial factor. It would indeed be surprising if this were not so because the whole process of socialization in childhood is an influence situation in which the child learns to make those decisions for which he or she receives approval. The reward/cost system is established early and must remain a powerful influencing factor throughout life. Cooley (1929) called primary groups, such as the family, 'the nursery of human nature'.

However much the presence of others affects the decision-making process, the first consideration must be that there is something to influence. In this sense individuals make decisions and others agree or disagree. Committees as decision-making groups demonstrate quite clearly that there are some committee members who appear to be much more skillful in gaining acceptance for their ideas than other members. Equally, they also demonstrate that a group of members with similar degrees of skill often produce decisions that are sheer compromise.

Clearly, decision making is not based upon the objective assessment of the available data, a state of affairs that often accounts for the incredulity with which decisions are received by those who will be affected by them. Sometimes the only available explanation seems to be that sheer bloodymindedness has been the basis of the decision when, in fact, many influences unknown, certainly to the recipients of the decision and often enough to the deciders, have affected the outcome. A whole hidden agenda of complex and perhaps only partially understood sets of responses based on personal assessment of the situation, on past experience, and upon desired outcomes, has gone into the way the decision has emerged.

The prospect is frightening as long as the standard of self-awareness remains low. Decisions will be affected by group influences that are not apparent; they will be made with all sincerity as objectively based on available data, and yet they will be the result of the interaction of a complex mesh of motivations and perceptions, of considerations, of possible consequences, and of awareness of some pressures and of ignorance of others. Improved decision making can only emerge from increased clarity of understanding of the group and other pressures involved and by attempting to allow for their effects. Otherwise essential decision making has to be left to individuals who then shoulder enormous responsibility for their decisions, but who may have clear enough vision to make choices quickly and who thus have been the preferred means of decision making in terms of urgent crisis.

LEARNING

'People devalue their emotions and consider them to be inappropriate in problem solving or work situations, for fear of alienating a friend or of losing a promotion, perhaps even a job. In the process, however, they become emotionally malnutritioned and lose a bit of their humanity.'

(Blumberg and Golembiewski 1976 : 25)

Despite the clumsy English used here, Blumberg and Golembiewski are writing about the way people learn to devalue an enormous and very valuable area of themselves and of their experience so that their learning becomes related almost exclusively to the rational and intellectual elements of personality. Yet there is no evidence to console us that such self-deprivation produces either better learners or better people. On the contrary, it would seem only too clear that ignoring the emotions does not at all diminish their influence upon rational thinking, but creates an extra difficulty in that their effect becomes covert and there-fore largely unappreciated by the person concerned. This is one reason for the huge expansion of methods for indirectly bringing home to people the appearance of their behaviour to others and the perceived consequences of it. The whole area of learning about the hidden influences on behaviour has to come from without, under conditions in which the information will be accepted as valid.

By far the most accessible, and probably the most effective, of these methods is to create a group in which the level of trust is such that each member will accept from the others as an honest assessment, feedback about how his or her behaviour is seen. This creates something of a circular argument that I believe it will be to our advantage to explore. 'Circular' may not be the correct adjective because the sequence we need to look at shows not so much a continuous movement that eventually feeds into itself but rather more a state of reciprocity.

If feedback from fellow group members is given in a climate of support in which acceptance is a likely outcome, then logically it can be argued that the individual's original 'blind state' must have been created by a similar situation. The appalling lack of recognition of the place and effect of emotion in decision making, so forcefully described by Blumberg and Golembiewski, is as much a result of group pressure as the learning with which it is hoped to remedy the situation. When people describe as 'com-mon sense' the fact that children and adults also learn better from teachers they like, why is it so difficult to recognize that in this item of so-called common sense is the recognition that learning is affected by the emotional state of the learner and his or her perception of the learning situation? Can it be that to admit such an obvious fact generates fear, a fear that we do not conform to the expected image of clear, rational thinking people, that we are not as objective, or as much in control as the accepted stereotype would suggest, that the criteria we use for making sense of our world are no more absolute than anything else, and that in reality we are only accepting points of reference *as if* they were fixed and immutable? If so, the greatest relief from this fear must be the

realization that others believe almost as we do; they confirm our
as if reference points and seem to offer the evidence of numbers
of their actual truth. But no matter how many people affirm
something that is not actually so, it does not alter its reality one
jot, whatever psychological effect it may have upon those who
make the assertions – unless, of course, one believes there is no
objective reality beyond the perceptions of human beings.

Perhaps the greatest contribution that group influence can
bring to the process of learning is to create situations in which
individuals can begin to appreciate the kind of influence group
pressures can have on learning and incidentally in other spheres.
In other words, group experience of a given kind can reveal the
group processes at work; learning about what seriously affects
learning can be achieved.

DESIGN IN 'CREATED' GROUPS

All 'created' groups are artificially constructed entities. The conflict between creation, a deliberate act backed by intelligence and
reason, and the freedom to behave in a spontaneous, self-
learning situation where control is vested in all members,
appears to be absolute. It is what de Maré (1972) calls 'the
untenable paradox of being made to be spontaneously democratic'. If the group's power ultimately resides in the fact that its
members can gain some understanding of the resources available
for their use providing they can create a situation in which those
resources become not only available but usable, then the factors
that govern the effective design of groups become clear. This is
not to say that they become easy to manipulate, but they can
provide a serious guide. The problems are still great, even when
acceptance is made that such a guide exists.

The first problem lies in the analysis of what need exists. This
is in itself difficult enough. How clearly can we define the
constituents of a situation? All the definitions we tend to use are
global, e.g. 'we need to weigh the available evidence and make a
decision', or 'we need to improve the chances of these people to
gain personal growth'.

The simple analysis of 'natural' groups shows that what emerges as the group's structure and function is significantly different for each of the five groups that were looked at (the family, friendship and work groups, teams, and committees), showing that the design of each group used different combinations and intensities of group processes and other 'factors-affecting' to achieve efficiency. Even here the analysis had to be conducted in terms of wide generalizations because of the variety of functions of the groups considered. Where groups become more function-specific, the combinations and intensities of the 'factors-affecting' can also be discerned with increased clarity.

So the crude nature of our ability to define need also makes the problem of matching processes that meet that need a comparatively rough process. The success that 'created' groups achieve must lie in the fact that all groups possess the processes needed to meet all situations in which they are used. But how wasteful such hit or miss methods are is shown by the large number of 'created' groups that do not survive long enough for the necessary patterns of 'factors-affecting' to emerge, or only achieve a small part of what would have been possible because energy had to be used dealing with factors among which neither discrimination, priority, nor value could be established early enough.

'The group circle is itself a system composed of individual components who, through a communication and meta-communication, reshape by a process of "morphogenesis" a meta-structure according to the information it emits, and which is experienced by the individual as having a particular meaning characteristic of that particular meta-structure . . . at that particular place and moment.'   (de Maré 1972 : 149)

What kind of information do we want a particular group to emit about itself ? What kind of people, possessing what kind of characteristics, will generate the information that will change their group system or their perception of it into an instrument that will achieve the goals allotted to it? How can we influence the situation so that the necessary information is actually emitted? These and many other questions like them lead to the structuring

of detailed designs for particular groups because the answers to
them suggest the elements that should be combined. We have to
design a system in which participation is possible, in which a
common language can develop, in which common values govern
behaviour, and in which all that is meant by shared experience
gives to each group member a social matrix, an instrument that is
familiar and predictable, safe and usable, and that ultimately
generates increased satisfactions. Links have to be forged across
the spaces that separate people.

One of the starting points of this book was the discussion of
time in the introduction. Let us now consider time as an element
of design. The kind of links discussed here take time to develop,
so time is a very important variable in group design. Families last
for ever; friendship groups are often quite short-lived, but can
last a life-time; teams also do not last long; and committees, too,
tend to be of short duration. The time element is related to
function. The friendship group has a clear element of similarity
among members that starts them off at a level of cohesion that
other groups would have to develop slowly through a process of
creating the kind of group in which it became possible. The time
that committees need is related to (a) the nature of the decisions
they have to make, e.g. one-off or ongoing, (b) the amount of
information they are presented with, and (c) the characteristics of
the members.

Time can be used intensively as in Marathon groups, or
intermittently as in a group meeting held once a week. But the
effects of intensity and sporadicity, while not the same, have
sufficient similarity to be substitutes where circumstances dictate. The time needed for a group to achieve its aims must be
'designed' into its programme, which implies that group designers should know how long the desired outcome will take given
their current circumstances.

McGrath and Altman, writing about the deficiency of research
into what they call 'temporal aspects' of small groups, said:

'Temporal relationships of at least three kinds are of concern in
small group research: (1) temporal aspects of the group's

"pre-study history" (2) directional changes in the group
through time – "between-session" patterns of group development and (3) phasic, cyclical, or sequential fluctuations in
group activity through time – "within-session" patterns of
group process.'   (McGrath and Altman 1966 :72)

Time is one of the more obvious design elements in small
'created' groups, and most people working with such groups
would probably take cognizance of its significance. But the
known evidence of its effect as a constraint is not vast and in
many cases the other 'factors-affecting' are even less well
covered. More information is needed so that the elements of
group design can be used more effectively and not left to the
wasteful process of selection by the attrition and subsequent
abandoning of unwanted elements.

All the other 'factors-affecting' are also related to function and
their value lies in two principal areas. First, they define areas of
group behaviour and some of the influences that act upon them,
so they can be used to analyse existing groups. Thus, I have
presented the 'factors-affecting', showing their origins and some
of the principal ideas in which they are embedded, and then used
them to make an analysis of five kinds of more-or-less naturally
occurring groups.

Second, the 'factors-affecting' can be used as the basic elements of group design when specific knowledge of need exists.
So, in Part Three I have tried to show how certain created groups
have used these design elements and with what effect. This
inevitably leads to the conclusion that most creators of groups
tend to concentrate on some design elements and ignore others.
This would be well enough if to ignore in this context meant not
to forget about but to allow for elements and effects. All design is
concerned as much with what to leave out as what to put in, but it
must also be concerned with assessing the cost of such selective
decisions. In groups the cost must always take into consideration
the ubiquitous nature of the 'factors-affecting' so that choosing
to emphasize some factors does not necessarily eliminate the
effect of the continued presence of others. What has to be

achieved is the best possible weighting in any given situation.

Finally, Part Four attempted to show briefly how the 'factors-affecting' showed up as influences, often unrecognized as such, in many aspects of everyday life. Lack of recognition implies exactly the problem mentioned in the last paragraph. In this case, many of the effects are attributed to other causes, e.g. sheer stubbornness, or unaccountable stupidity that do not increase the probability of human beings living in harmony, nor even of becoming more understanding.

It is possible for smallish groups of very different people to learn to live and work together in harmony and co-operation, but the design that generates such a situation has of necessity to be radically different from the 'design' of current society and so has to be artificially sustained. What people get from such situations is a recognition of what is possible and some transfer of learning to the larger society. But, as Part Three attempted to show, our efforts at design are seldom good; they are always imbalanced, and our understanding of the elements of design and their functions is poor. I am afraid that I do not have too much hope for anything but a continuing patchy and sporadic development in the future. We have a long, long way to go to master the art of Gathering Together.

REFERENCES

Advisory Council on Child Care (DHSS) (1970) Care and Treatment in a Planned Environment. A Report on the Community Homes Project. London: HMSO.

Allen, V. L. (1965) Situational Factors in Conformity. In L. Berkowitz (ed.) *Advances in Experimental Psychology*, Vol. 2. London: Academic Press.

Andreski, S. (1974) *Social Sciences as Sorcery*. Harmondsworth: Penguin.

Argyle, M. (1969) *Social Interaction*. London: Methuen.

—— (1972) *The Social Psychology of Work*. Harmondsworth: Penguin.

Ariès, P. (1973) *Centuries of Childhood*. Harmondsworth: Penguin.

Aronson, E. (1976) *The Social Animal*. San Francisco: Freeman.

Bales, R. F. (1950) *Interaction Process Analysis: A Method for the Study of Small Groups*. Cambridge, Mass.: Addison-Wesley.

—— and Slater, P. E. (1955) Role Differentiation in Small Decision-Making Groups. In T. Parsons (ed.) *The Family, Socialization and Interaction Process*. New York: Free Press.

Bannister, D. (1969) A Psychology of Persons. *New Society* 4 December: 895–97.

Bennis, W. G. (1962) Goals and Meta-goals of Laboratory Education. *Human Relations Training News* **6**(3): 1–4.

—— (1966) *Changing Organizations*. New York: McGraw-Hill.

Berkowitz, L. and Green, J. A. (1962) The Stimulus Qualities of the Scapegoat. *Journal of Abnormal and Social Psychology* **64**: 293–301.

Berne, E. (1975) *What do you do after you say Hello? The Psychology of Human Destiny*. London: Corgi.

Bettelheim, B. (1969) *Children of the Dream*. London: Thames & Hudson.

Beukenkamp, C. (1952) Some Observations Made During Group Therapy. *Psychiatric Quarterly Supplement* **26**: 22–6.

Blau, P. M. and Scott, W. R. (1980) Who Benefits? In A. Etzioni and E. W. Lehman (eds) *A Sociological Reader on Complex Organizations*. New York: Holt, Rinehart & Winston.

Blumberg, A. and Golembiewski, R. T. (1976) *Learning and Change in Groups*. Harmondsworth: Penguin.

Bolton, N. (1976) *The Psychology of Thinking*. London: Methuen.

Bonner, H. (1959) *Group Dynamics: Principles and Applications*. New York: Ronald Press.

Bowen, M. (1966) The Use of Family Theory in Clinical Practice. *Comprehensive Psychiatry* **7**: 345–74.

Brown, J. A. C. (1954) *The Social Psychology of Industry*. Harmondsworth: Penguin.

Butler, S. (1663) *Hudibras*.

Button, L. (1974) *Developmental Groupwork with Adolescents*. London: University of London Press.

Canter, D. and Canter, S. (1979) *Designing for Therapeutic Environments: A Review of Research*. Chichester: John Wiley.

Cartwright, D. and Zander, A. (1953) *Group Dynamics: Research and Theory*. London: Tavistock.

Chapple, E. D. and Coon, C. S. (1965) The Equilibrium of Groups. In A. P. Hare, R. F. Bales, and E. F. Borgatta (eds) *Small Groups*. New York: Knopf.

Collins, B. E. and Guetzkow, H. (1964) *A Social Psychology of Group Processes for Decision-Making*. New York: John Wiley.

Cooley, C. H. (1929) *Social Organization*. New York: Scribner.

Davis, J. H. (1969) *Group Performance.* Reading, Mass.: Addison-Wesley.

Deutsch, M. and Gerard, H. B. (1955) A Study of Normative and Informational Influence Upon Individual Judgement. *Journal of Abnormal and Social Psychology* **51**: 629–36.

Douglas, T. (1976) *Groupwork Practice.* London: Tavistock.

—— (1979) *Groupwork Processes in Social Work.* Chichester: John Wiley.

Ellis, D. G., Werbel, W. S., and Fisher, B. A. (1978) Toward a Systemic Organisation of Groups. *Small Group Behaviour* **9**(4): 451ff.

Etzioni, A. (1980) Compliance Structures. In A. Etzioni and E. W. Lehman (eds) *A Sociological Reader on Complex Organizations.* New York: Holt, Reinhart & Winston.

Fairhead, S. (1981) *The Guardian.* 22 December.

Feldman, R. A. (1969) Group Integration: Intense Interpersonal Dislike and Social Groupwork Intervention. *Social Work* (US) **14**(3): 30–9.

Festinger, L. (1957) *A Theory of Cognitive Dissonance.* Stanford, Calif.: Stanford University Press.

Foulkes, S. H. and Anthony, E. J. (1957) *Group Psychotherapy.* Harmondsworth: Penguin.

Fraser, C. (1978) Small Groups; Structure and Leadership. In H. Tajfel and C. Fraser (eds) *Introducing Social Psychology.* Harmondsworth: Penguin.

French, J. R. P. and Raven, B. H. (1959) The Bases of Social Power. In D. Cartwright (ed.) *Studies in Social Power.* Ann Arbor, Mich.: Institute for Social Research, University of Michigan.

Gahagan, J. (1975) *Interpersonal and Group Behaviour.* London: Methuen.

Gide, A. (1903) *Concerning Influence in Literature.* Pretexts.

Gioscia, V. (1974) Editor's Statement. In A. E. Scheflen (ed.) *How Behaviour Means.* New York: Anchor/Doubleday.

Goffman, E. (1968) *Asylums: Essays on the Social Situation of Mental Patients and other Inmates.* Harmondsworth: Penguin.

—— (1969a) Insanity of Place. *Psychiatry* **32** : 357–88.

—— (1969b) *Presentation of Self in Everyday life.* Harmonds-worth: Penguin.

Golembiewski, R. T. (1962) *The Small Group.* Chicago: University of Chicago Press.

—— (1980) Organization Development in Industry: Perspectives on Progress and Slickness. In P. B. Smith (ed.) *Small Groups and Personal Change.* London: Methuen.

—— and Blumberg, A. (1970) *Sensitivity Training and the Laboratory Approach.* Itasca, Ill.: Peacock.

Grusky, O. and Pollner, M. (eds) (1981) *The Sociology of Mental Illness.* New York: Holt, Rinehart & Winston.

Hare, A. P. (1962) *Handbook of Small Group Research.* New York: Free Press.

Heap, K. (1977) *Group Theory for Social Workers: An Introduction.* Oxford: Pergamon.

Heisenberg, W. (1927) Uber den Anschaulichen Inhalt der Quantentheoratischen Kinematick und Mechanik. *Zeitschrift für Physik* **43** : 172

Hochbaum, G. M. (1954) The Relation between Group Members Self-Confidence and their Reactions to Group Pressures to Conformity. *American Sociological Review* **19** : 678–87.

Hoffman, L. R. (1965) Group Problem-Solving. In L. Berkowitz (ed.) *Advances in Experimental Psychology*, Vol. 2. London: Academic Press.

Holmes, T. H. and Rahe, R. H. (1967) The Social Readjustment Rating Scale. *Journal of Psychosomatic Research* **2** : 213–18.

Home Office (1970) *Care and Treatment in a Planned Environment: A Report on the Community Homes Project.* London: HMSO.

Janis, I. L. (1972) *Victims of Groupthink: A Psychological Study of Foreign Policy Decisions and Fiascoes.* Boston: Houghton Mifflin.

Jones, C. S. (1967) In the Midst of Life. In E. A. Gollman (ed.) *Explaining Death to Children.* Boston: Beacon Press.

Jones, K. (1967) The Development of Institutional Care. In

Association of Social Workers *New Thinking About Institutional Care*. London: Association of Social Workers.

Jones, M. (1979) The Therapeutic Community Social Learning and Social Change. In R. D. Hinshelwood and N. Manning (eds) *Therapeutic Communities*. London: Routledge & Kegan Paul.

Kelly, G. A. (1970) A Brief Introduction to Personal Construct Theory. In D. Bannister (ed.) *Perspectives in Personal Construct Theory*. New York: Academic Press.

Kelman, H. C. (1950) Effects of Success and Failure on 'Suggestibility' in Autokinetic Situation. *Journal of Abnormal and Social Psychology* **45** : 267–85.

Kenny, M. (1981) *Daily Telegraph*. 11 July.

Killilea, M. (1976) Mutual Help Organizations: Interpretations in the Literature. In G. Caplan and M. Killilea (eds) *Support Systems and Mutual Help: Multidisciplinary Explorations*. New York: Grune & Stratton.

Laing, R. D. and Esterson, A. (1970) *Sanity, Madness and the Family*. Harmondsworth: Penguin.

Langley, R. and Levy, R. C. (1977) *Wife Beating – The Silent Crisis*. New York: Simon & Schuster.

Levanway, R. W. (1972) *Advanced General Psychology*. Philadelphia: Davis.

Lewin, K. (1947) Group Decision and Social Change. In T. M. Newcomb and E. L. Hartley (eds) *Readings in Social Psychology*. New York: Henry Holt.

Litvak, E. (1967) Communication Theory and Group Factors. In E. Thomas (ed.) *Behavioural Science for Social Workers*. New York: Free Press.

Lowenstein, E. R. (1971) Group Size and Decision-Making Committees: Some Inferences from the Behavioural Sciences. *Applied Social Studies* **3** (2) : 107–16.

Lundberg, G. A. and Lawsing, M. (1937) The Sociography of Some Community Relations. *American Sociological Review* June: 318–35.

Maier, H. W. (1961) Group Living: A Unique Feature in Residential Treatment. In *New Perspectives on Services to*

Groups: Theory, Organization and Practice. New York: National Association of Social Workers.

Mann, R. D. (1967) *Interpersonal Styles and Group Development.* New York: John Wiley.

Maré, P. B. de (1972) *Perspectives in Group Psychotherapy.* London: Allen & Unwin.

—— and Kreger, L. C. (1974) *Introduction to Group Treatments in Psychiatry.* London: Butterworth.

Margulies, N. and Raia, A. (1979) *Conceptual Foundations of Organization Development.* New York: McGraw-Hill.

McGrath, J. I. and Altman, I. (1966) *Small Group Research.* New York: Holt, Rinehart & Winston.

Medcof, J. and Roth, J. (1979) *Approaches to Psychology.* Milton Keynes: Open University Press.

Milgram, S. (1974) *Obedience to Authority.* New York: Harper & Row.

Miller, F. D. (1976) The Problem of Transfer of Training in Learning Groups: Group Cohesion as an End in Itself. *Small Group Behaviour* **7** (2) : 221–36.

Miller, G. A. (1969a) *The Psychology of Communication.* Harmondsworth: Penguin.

—— (1969b) Psychology as a Means of Promoting Human Welfare. *American Psychologist* 1064–075.

Miller, H. (1941) The Alcoholic Veteran with the Washboard Cranium. *The Wisdom of the Heart.*

Millham, S., Bullock, R., and Hosie, K. (1980) *Learning to Care: The Training of Staff for Residential Social Work with Children.* Farnborough: Gower.

——, and Haak, F. (1981) *Issues of Control in Residential Child Care.* London: HMSO.

Morrice, J. K. W. (1979) Basic Concepts: A Critical Review. In R. D. Hinshelwood and N. Manning (eds) *Therapeutic Communities: Reflections and Progress.* London: Routledge & Kegan Paul.

Newman, P. R. (1976) Analysis of Social Interaction as an Environmental Variable. *Small Group Behaviour* **7** (1) : 44.

Nicholson, J. (1977) *Habits.* London: Macmillan.

Paul, G. L. (1967) Strategy of Outcome Research in Psycho-therapy. *Journal of Consulting Psychology* **31** : 109–18.

Postle, D. (1980) *Catastrophe Theory*. Glasgow: Fontana.

Rahe, R. H. (1972) Subjects' Recent Life Changes and their Near-future Illness Susceptibility. *Advances in Psycho-somatic Medicine* **8** : 2–19.

Raven, B. H. and Rubin, J. Z. (1976) *Social Psychology: People in Groups*. New York: John Wiley.

Robinson, D. (1980) Self-Help Health Groups. In P. B. Smith (ed.) *Small Groups and Personal Change*. London: Methuen.

Roethlisberger, F. J. and Dickson, W. J. (1939) *Management and the Worker*. Cambridge, Mass.: Harvard University Press.

Rosenthal, W. A. (1973) Social Group Theory. *Social Work* **18** (51) : 60–6.

Runcie, J. F. (1973) Group Formation: Theoretical and Empirical Approaches. *Small Group Behaviour* **4** (2) : 181–205.

Russell, B. (1946) *History of Western Philosophy*. London: Allen & Unwin.

Sallust (86–34BC) *Catiline*.

Satir, V. (1967) *Conjoint Family Therapy: A Guide to Theory and Technique*. Palo Alto, Calif.: Science & Behaviour Books.

Scheflen, A. E. (1974) *How Behaviour Means*. New York: Anchor.

Schur, E. M. (1979) *Interpreting Deviance: A Sociological Intro-duction*. New York: Harper & Row.

Schutz, W. C. (1959) *F.I.R.O.* New York: Holt, Rinehart & Winston.

Selye, H. (1976) *The Stress of Life*. New York: McGraw-Hill.

Shaw, M. E. (1971) *Group Dynamics: The Psychology of Small Group Behaviour*. New York: McGraw-Hill.

—— (1974) *An Overview of Small Group Behaviour*. Morris-town, NJ: General Learning Press.

Sherif, C. W. (1976) *Orientation in Social Psychology*. New York: Harper & Row.

Sherif, M. (1936) *The Psychology of Social Norms*. New York: Harper & Row.

Siegel, A. E. and Siegel, S. (1957) Reference Groups, Membership Groups and Attitude Change. *Journal of Abnormal and Social Psychology* **55** : 360–64.

Simon, H. A. (1969) *The Science of the Artificial*. Cambridge, Mass.: MIT Press.

Smith, D. (1978) Dyadic Encounter: The Foundation of Dialogue and the Group Process. *Small Group Behaviour* **9**(2) : 287–304.

Smith, P. B. (1971) The Varieties of Group Experience. *New Society* March: 483–85.

—— (ed.) (1980) *Small Groups and Personal Change*. London: Methuen.

——, Wood, H., and Smale, G. G. (1980) The Usefulness of Groups in Clinical Settings. In P. B. Smith (ed.) *Small Groups and Personal Change*. London: Methuen.

Sprott, W. J. (1952) *Social Psychology*. London: Methuen.

—— (1958) Human Groups. Harmondsworth: Penguin.

Stebbing, S. L. (1939) *Thinking to Some Purpose*. Harmondsworth: Penguin.

Steiner, I. D. (1974) *Task-performing Groups*. Morristown, NJ: General Learning Press.

Szasz, T. (1961) *The Myth of Mental Illness*. New York: Haber-Harper.

Tajfel, H. (1969) Cognitive Aspects of Prejudice. *Journal of Social Issues* **25** : 79–97.

—— and Fraser, C. (eds) (1978) *Introducing Social Psychology*. Harmondsworth: Penguin

Thom, R. (1980) Structural Stability and Morphogenesis. In D. Postle (ed.) *Catastrophe Theory*. Glasgow: Fontana.

Torrance, E. P. (1954) Some Consequences of Power Differences on Decision-Making in Permanent and Temporary Three-Man Groups. *Research Studies* **22** : 130–40.

Vinter, R. D. (1967) The Essential Components of Group Work Practice. In R. D. Vinter (ed.) *Readings in Group Work Practice*. Ann Arbor, Mich.: Campus.

Walker, T. G. (1974) Decision-making Superiority of Groups. *Small Group Behaviour* **5**(1) : 121.

Watson, L. (1979) *Life Tide*. London: Hodder & Stoughton.

Whitehorn, K. (1982) *The Observer*. 24 January.

Whiteley, J. S. and Gordon, J. (1979) *Group Approaches in Psychiatry*. London: Routledge & Kegan Paul.

Whyte, W. H. (1960) *The Organisation Man*. Harmondsworth: Penguin.

Wittgenstein, L. (1953) *Philosophical Investigations*. Oxford: Blackwell.

Yalom, I. D. (1970) *The Theory and Practice of Group Psychotherapy*. New York: Basic Books.

INDEX

activity: committee, 145; friendship groups, 108–10; team, 131–32
adolescent friendship groups, 100–01
affection, *see* liking
aims of book, 11–13
Allen, V. L., 44–5, 70, 125
Altman, I., 62, 79, 236–37
altruism, 193
Andreski, S., 7
Anthony, E. J., 191
Argyle, M., 11, 77–8, 83, 90, 100–01, 103, 113, 125, 141
Ariès, P., 84–6, 88
Aronson, E., 42–3, 45, 66, 149, 227, 230
artificiality, 163–64, 178
attitudes, 219–21
attraction, 100–01; *see also* liking

balance, family, 95–7
Bales, R. F., 65–6
Bannister, D., 15
Barnard, C. I., 115
basic group processes, 64
behaviour, human, 5–7: and environment, 156–57; modification, 156, 189–90, 194
behavioural science, 5–8
beliefs, 219–21
beneficiaries, 162
Bennis, W. G., 120
Berkowitz, L., 227
Berne, E., 212
Bettelheim, B., 86
Beukencamp, C., 86
Blau, P. M., 162
Blumberg, A., 198, 200, 232–33
Bolton, N., 25, 27
Bonner, H., 71
Bowen, M., 86
Brown, J. A. C., 40, 115
Butler, S., 45
Button, L., 103, 107

Canter, D. and Canter, S., 182–83, 186, 188
care in residential institutions, 164–66
Cartwright, D., 36
catharsis, 194
change: in 'created' groups, 190–95; in family, 89–90
Chapple, E. D., 97
childhood, 84
climate: committee, 144; family, 92; friendship groups, 108; group processes, 64; team, 129
closed groups, 93
co-operation, 49; team, 123, 125
co-ordination, team, 130
cognitive dissonance, 44
cohesion, 64; committee, 144; family, 92; friendship groups, 107–09; team, 128–29; work organizations, 116–17, 222
cohesiveness: in 'created' groups, 194, 196; in work organizations, 116
'collective', 32
Collins, B. E., 62, 79
competition, 49–51
committees, 82, 138–52; group processes of, 141–48
communication, 69–71; in committees, 141–42; in family, 94; in reference groups, 217; in work organizations, 114–15
companionship levels, 103–05
competition, 126, 132
compliance, 45–7, 161
conflict: and consensus, 221–23; team, 132, 134–35; in work organizations, 121–22
conformity, 42–5, 69–71; in committees, 144; in 'created' groups, 200; in reference groups, 216–17; in residential institutions, 159; in therapeutic community, 180–81

consensus and conflict, 221–23
constraints, 73; nature of, 50–4; therapeutic community, 176
consultation, 119
context: of book, 4–9; relationship to, 182–83
contract: committee, 146; team, 136
convenience of residential institutions, 167–68
Cooley, C. H., 231
Coon, C. S., 97
cost: of 'created' groups, 205; of residential institutions, 174
'created' groups, 10, 37–40, 55, 189–205; change in, 190–95; design in, 234–38; stability and support in, 195–201; understanding, 27
custodial institutions, 164–66, 201–03

data collection, 23–5
Davis, J. H., 79
decision making, 64, 77, 230–32; committee, 139–41, 143; family, 91; team, 128; work organizations, 118–19
definitions: of groups, 33–40; of residential institutions, 161–71; of therapeutic communities, 178–88
dependence, team, 125–26, 134
description: of groups, 29–55; of group processes, 62–71
design: in 'created' groups, 234–38; possibilities of therapeutic communities, 181–85
Deutsch, M., 70
development: family, 89–90; friendship groups, 106; team, 127
deviance, 228
Dickson, W. J., 112
differences in ethnic groups, 227–28
dissonance, cognitive, 44
Douglas, T., 17, 50–1, 58, 63, 69, 203
dramaturgical theory of behaviour, 215
duration constraint, 51
dyadic interaction, 70–1, 94–6, 225
dynamics, family, 88–94

Ellis, D. G., 186
embedding, 203–04
emotional problems, 148–50
emotions and learning, 232–33; see also liking

enhancing conditions, committee, 140, 146–47
environment: behaviour and, 156–57; committee, 144; constraint, 50, 52; family, 92; friendship groups, 108; residential institutions, 172; team, 129; therapeutic community, 176–78, 186–88
equilibrium, group, 96–8
Esterson, A., 224
ethnic groups, 226–30
Etzioni, A., 161–62
existence: data collection, 23–5; explanations of, 25–8; making sense of, 25–8
experts, 179–80
explanations of existence, 25–8

'factors-affecting', 68, 71–4, 150–51, 237–38; 'created' groups, 192; friendship groups, 105–10; residential institutions, 171–75; therapeutic communities, 183, 186
family, 4, 81, 83–99; distinctive nature of, 86–8; dyadic interaction, 94–6; dynamics of, 88–94; group equilibrium, 96–8; recapitulation of, 193–94; as reference group, 216
feedback, 10, 225, 233
Feldman, R. A., 227
Festinger, L., 44, 213
formal group, 141–42
Foulkes, S. H., 191
Fraser, C., 79, 103, 226, 231
French, J. R. P., 46
frequency of occurrence of group processes, 61–2
friendship groups, 81, 100–10; group processes, 105–10; nature of, 101–04
functions of groups, 79, 160

Gahagan, J., 29, 101–02
Gerard, H. B., 70
Gide, A., 40
Gioscia, V., 209, 215
goals: committee, 143; family, 91; formation, 64; friendship groups, 107; team, 128; work organizations, 121
Goffman, E., 133, 167, 169, 172–73, 215, 221
Golembiewski, R. T., 33, 120, 198, 200, 232–33

Gordon, J., 86, 195
Green, J. A., 227
group: concept, arbitrary nature of, 31–3; development, 64, 142; described and defined, 29–55
group processes, 1–4, 15–74; description of, 29–55, 62–71; existence, making sense of, 18–28; in committees, 141–48; in 'created' groups, 192–94; in family, 88–98; in friendship groups, 105–10; identification of, 58–62; in 'natural' groups, 77–152; in special environments, 155–238; in teams, 133–36; in work organizations, 115–21
'groupthink', 230
Grusky, O., 223
Guetzkow, H., 26, 62, 79

Hare, A. P., 79
Hawthorne Experiment, 112
Heap, K., 37
Heisenberg, W., 19
Hochbaum, G. M., 54
Hoffman, L. R., 105, 139–40
Holmes, T. H., 184
hope, 193

identification: group, 47; of group processes, 58–62
implications, major, 209–38; decision making, 230–32; design in 'created' groups, 234–38; ethnic groups, 226–30; formation, maintenance, and change of attitudes, opinions, beliefs and values, 219–21; learning, 232–34; mental illness, 223–26; reference groups, 215–18; social consensus and conflict, 221–23
improvement, 183–84; see also behaviour modification
individual, 79, 81, 178–81, 189
influence, 64; group, nature of, 40–50; in committee, 144; in family, 92; in friendship group, 107–08; in team, 129
information, imparting of, 192–93, 196
informational influences, 70
injustice, social, 210
intensity, 51, 150–52
interaction, 64–7; committee, 141–42;

family, 88–90; friendship group, 105; team, 126; work organization, 118–21
Interaction Process Analysis, 66
interdependency, team, 125–27, 134
internalization, group, 47–8
isolation, 168–69
Israel, 86–8

Janis, J. L., 230
Jones, C. S., 164
Jones, K., 171, 173
Jones, M., 176
justice, social, 210

Kelly, G. A., 179, 213
Kelman, H. C., 54
Kenny, M., 85
kibbutz, 86–8
Killilea, M., 196
knowledge of being human, 7–9
Kreger, L. C., 185

Laing, R. D., 224
Langley, R., 209
language, problem of, 27–8
Lawsing, M., 100
LCE, see logically consistent explanation
leadership: committee, 145–46, 149; constraints, 52–4; 'created' groups, 197; family, 93; friendship groups, 108–09; group processes, 3, 69, 72–3; residential institutions, 162, 164; team, 132
learning, 232–34
Levanway, R. W., 79, 226
Levy, R. C., 209
Lewin, K., 221
'Life-Scripts', 212–13
liking: in family, 163; in friendship groups, 100–02, 106, 109; in work organizations, 114, 116
Litvak, E., 69, 221
locomotive group processes, 64
logically consistent explanations of existence, 25–8
Lowenstein, E. R., 148
loyalty, 109, 129, 222
Lundberg, G. A., 100

McGrath, J. I., 62, 79, 236–37
Maier, H. W., 163

maintenance in 'created' groups, 189–90, 196
Mann, R. D., 182
Maré, P. B. de, 58, 185, 234–35
Margulies, N., 120
marriage, 85; *see also* family
Medcof, J., 23
membership: committee, 144–45; friendship group, 108; group, 48–9; residential institutions, 172–73; team, 129–30
mental illness, 214, 223–26
Milgram, S., 42, 46
Miller, F. D., 169
Miller, G. A., 4–6, 21, 33
Miller, H., 52
Millham, S., 158
molar group processes, 64
Morrice, J. K. W., 178

natural' groups, 10–11, 27, 36–40, 55, 235; committees as, 138–52; family as, 83–99; friendship groups as, 100–10; teams as, 123–37; work organizations as, 112–22
nature of groups, 29–55; friendship groups, 101–04; teams, 125–33
Newman, P. K., 156
Nicholson, J., 100–01, 111
non-orthogonal nature of group processes, 60–1
non-verbal communication, 142
normative influences, 70
norms: committee, 143; family, 91–2; group processes, 64; team, 128; work organizations, 117–18

open groups, 131, 145, 176
operating constraints, 171–75
opinions, 219–21
Organizational Development programmes, 113, 121

Paul, G. L., 155
peer groups, 104, 218; *see also* friendship groups
performance, group, 78–9, 150, 152
Personal Construct Theory, 213
personal growth groups, 136
Pollner, M., 223
Postle, D., 23, 56
pressure, group, 64
prisons, 201–03

problem-solving group: committee as, 139–41, 143; team as, 125, 134; *see also* task-oriented
problems: with LCEs, 27–8; of therapeutic communities, 185–88
processes, *see* group processes
processing of people, 162, 165
productivity in work organizations, 119–21
psychotherapy, 191–92
punitive institutions, 169–71, 201–03
purpose: group processes, 64; teams, 125–33

Raia, A., 120
Raven, B. H., 46, 66, 80, 230
reality, definition of, 69
reference groups, 48–9, 215–18
relationships, 189, 193–94; *see also* liking
research data, 5–6
residential institutions, 158–75; defined, 161–71; operating constraints, 171–75
resources: committee, 145; 'created' groups, 190; family, 93; team, 130–31
restoration of equilibrium, 97
retarding conditions, committee, 139–40, 147–48
return to community, 178, 200
risk-taking, 143
rivalry, 148–50
Robinson, D., 197
Roethlisberger, F. J., 112
Roth, J., 23
Rubin, J. Z., 66, 80, 230
Runcie, J. F., 226
Russell, B., 58

Sallust, 100
Satir, V., 94
satisfaction, 112–13
Scheflen, A. E., 21, 212, 215
Schur, E. M., 42
Schutz, W. C., 106
Scott, W. K., 162
selection: in family, 94; in friendship group, 109–10; in team, 132–33
self, 48–9
self-help groups, 196–97, 218
sense of existence, 18–28

set, *see* team
'shared experience', 114
Shaw, M. E., 35, 43, 79
Sherif, C. W., 45, 48, 214, 216
Siegel, A. E. and Siegel, S., 48
similarity, 110, 227–29
Simon, H. A., 38
size: of committee, 145, 148, 150; of friendship group, 108; of team, 131; of work organization, 118–19
Smale, G. G., 192
Smith, D., 71, 94
Smith, P. B., 31, 80, 155, 192, 195, 197
'social anchor', 216
social: behaviour, 212–18, 221; conflict, 221–23; engineering, 27; evolution, 78; influences, 70; structure, 64; *see also* behaviour
socialization, 159, 194
solidarity, team, 135
special environments: in 'created' groups, 189–205; group processes in, 155–205; residential institutions, 158–75; therapeutic environments, 176–88
Sprott, W. J., 49, 189
standards, 64; committee, 143; family, 91–2; team, 128
status, 179–80
Stebbing, S. L., 219
Steiner, I. D., 54, 140
structural group processes, 64
structure: committee, 142; family, 90; friendship groups, 106; residential institutions, 173–75; team, 127
sub-groups, 64, 68; committee, 142–43; family, 90–1; friendship, 106–07; residential institutions, 161; team, 127; therapeutic community, 182
success, team, 135
support groups, 196–97, 218
support in 'created' groups, 189–90, 195–201
supra-systems, 186, 203
Szasz, T., 224

T-groups, 136

Tajfel, H., 70, 79, 86, 209, 226
task-oriented groups, 102–03, 125; *see also* problem-solving groups
teams, 82, 123–37; group processes, 133–36; nature and process of, 125–33
therapeutic environments, 176–88; residential 166–67, 204
Thom, R., 56
time: and committees, 145, 149; constraint, 1–2, 50, 52; in 'created' groups, 194–95; and design element, 236–37; and family, 88–9, 93; and friendship groups, 101, 108; and 'natural' groups, 78; and residential institutions, 173; and teams, 130
Torrance, E. P., 54, 134
'translation', 8

uncertainty principle, 19
understanding: existence, 20–3; problems of, 8–9, 11–13
uniformity, 107
United States, 120, 230
universality, 193

'value theory', 231
values, 64, 219–21; committee, 143; family, 91–2; team, 128
verbal communication, 141–42
Vinter, R. D., 190

Walker, T. G., 80
Whitehorn, K., 218
Whiteley, J. S., 86, 195
Whyte, W. H., 37
Wittgenstein, L., 27
Wood, H., 192
work organizations, 82, 111–22, 218; group processes in, 115–21; as structures containing groups, 113–15
work, group, 80

Yalom, I. D., 86, 191–92

Zander, A., 36